HOLLYWOOD
LOVE STORIES

HOLLYWOOD
LOVE STORIES

*True love stories
from behind the silver screen*

☆

GILL PAUL

METRO BOOKS
NEW YORK

For Marion, Christina, and Ruby:
three generations of superstars.

METRO BOOKS
New York

An Imprint of Sterling Publishing
387 Park Avenue South
New York, NY 10016

This book was conceived, designed, and produced by

Ivy Press

210 High Street, Lewes, East Sussex, BN7 2NS, UK

Creative Director Peter Bridgewater

Publisher Susan Kelly

Art Director Wayne Blades

Senior Editor Jayne Ansell

Designer Andrew Milne

Picture Researcher Katie Greenwood

ISBN 978-1-4351-5479-7

For information about custom editions, special sales, and premium
and corporate purchases, please contact Sterling Special Sales at
800-805-5489 or specialsales@sterlingpublishing.com.

Manufactured in China

Color origination by Ivy Press Reprographics

2 4 6 8 10 9 7 5 3 1

www.sterlingpublishing.com

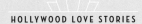

CONTENTS

MEMO

TO: Claude Binyon

DATE

SUBJECT: Carole Lombard — Please tell us
everything you know about her

FROM: The Office of the Editor

Subject: *Lombard*

BY CLAUDE BINYON

THE man asked me to write about
Lombard, star of RKO's "My
Night," and I said yes. He
knew her and I said yes. Then he
New York and left me in California.
ble in my brain.
Sure, I knew Carole Lombard
like you knew somebody you met
resort and can't remember whether
Iowa or Wisconsin, or whether you
send a post card or never up to
get married.
I wrote one picture for her

as a mother-in-law's kiss. The cabin where we
would have dinner was two miles away, through
sand and sand and mud and sand.
MacMurray stood up finally and stretched,
and his teeth chattered a message to pneumonia.
"be said, "who'd pay money to sit
in a hole."

Lombard

LIFE

AMERICAN BOY'S ADVENTURE WITH AN AFRICAN TRIBE

BLAZING NEW PAGE IN THE LEGEND OF LIZ

RICHARD BURTON
WITH ELIZABETH TAYLOR
ON CLEOPATRA SET

ALSO THIS WEEK

Where NOT To Eat
When You're Out Driving

Australia Sets Sail
for America's Cup

TRIUMPH OF A SON'S FAITH IN HIS FATHER
by ROBERT WALLACE

APRIL 13 · 1962 · 20¢

Spe
TR
Katha
HE

KE

Hollywood marriages are notoriously precarious and always have been. Gossip columns and newspaper headlines trumpet the beginnings of affairs, quote the happy couple as they declare undying love, print the radiant wedding photographs, and then start counting down the days till it all falls apart. Mickey Rooney, Lana Turner, and Elizabeth Taylor each married eight times, and the average movie star of the "Golden Age of Hollywood" (usually dated from the first talkie in 1927 through to around 1948–49) has been married around three or four times. Why should the divorce rate be so high when actors are human beings who need love as much as the rest of us—perhaps even more so?

THE EARLY YEARS

The movie industry was born on December 28, 1895, when thirty-five audience members sat in Paris's Grand Café to watch a short film by the Lumière Brothers. The medium was a novelty hit but it wasn't enticing to theater actors, who considered it beneath their dignity to appear on celluloid. Actors who couldn't find other work consented to be in early films but didn't want their names in the credits. However, the public soon became fascinated by the performers and gave them nicknames: Florence Lawrence was "The Biograph Girl" because she worked for Biograph Studios; Mary Pickford was "Little Mary" after the child she played on-screen; and Max Aronson was "Bronco Billy" in a series of films about that character.

In 1911, *Photoplay magazine* and *Motion Picture Story* were founded to give readers the inside scoop on new films in production, and in 1914 Louella Parsons wrote her first gossip column. They understood what the movie bosses were trying to deny—that the public had a hunger for information about the private lives of these beautiful people. It also became apparent that the fans would be faithful to their favorites and would pay to see all their films, providing a ready-made audience. So far, so good, but the bosses were nervous about giving actors pumped-up ideas of their own worth. They didn't want popular actors being able to demand higher salaries, which could

BELOW
Florence Lawrence, The Biograph Girl. Her fame was assured after a publicity stunt in which the studio spread a rumor she had died in an automobile accident, then took out a full-page newspaper ad announcing that she was still alive and had a new movie coming out.

MISS FLORENCE LAWRENCE
(LUBIN)

ABOVE
Photoplay Magazine,
November 1914, and
Motion Picture Story,
September 1911. These
magazines described
movies in production
and ran features on
the stars' lives.

undermine the films' profit margins. Accordingly, they tied them to contracts that provided a weekly salary for a period of, several years. The studio could pull the plug if box-office receipts for a particular star were not up to expectations, but the actors were stuck with the studio till the end of the term.

By the early 1920s, the studio bosses' minds were focused on another problem—the behavior of their stars. When they brought together some very attractive people in the feverish environment of a movie set and asked them to play love scenes, lo and behold, they started having affairs with each other. Some even left their marriages for each other—and this in an era when divorcees were ostracized in polite society. Many also seemed to drink and party rather a lot, reveling in their newfound celebrity, and a string of sex and drug scandals hit the press. This was the kind of negative publicity that it was thought could ruin the whole industry.

THIS YEAR'S LOVE MARKET... Its Highs

ILLUSTRATION BY JOANNE ADAMS

ABOVE
*A 1939 illustration
of romantic liaisons
in Hollywood, both
rumored (such as Greta
Garbo and conductor
Leopold Stokowski,
Tyrone Power and Sonja
Henie/Janet Gaynor)
and those that led
to marriage (all except
for Howard Hughes and
Katharine Hepburn).*

From that time on, actors continued to cause headaches for studio bosses, giving them two major challenges: how to keep their stars on the straight and narrow (or hush up any misdemeanors if they strayed); and how to keep them from having too much power over their own careers. Attempting to solve these problems was like trying to herd cats.

THE STAR SYSTEM

During the 1920s, five major studios were established in Hollywood—MGM, Paramount, Warner Brothers, Twentieth Century Fox, and RKO—along with a few smaller ones, including Columbia, Universal, and United Artists. Each had its own producers and directors, its own back lot where most of the films were shot, and its own roster of actors and crew on long-term contracts. To win such a contract was the dream of boys and girls across America, and magazines published lists of locations where talent scouts hung out so that would-be actors could put on their best clothes and hang around hopefully. If noticed, an actor might be sent to Hollywood for a screen test and, if you seemed photogenic enough, you would soon be hustled into the studio production line. Acting ability had little to do with it, but a willingness to go to the "casting couch" was a definite bonus in many studios.

Many changes were required of actors. First, the name might be changed: Lucille Fay LeSueur became Joan Crawford, while Archibald Alexander Leach became Cary Grant. Next, overall appearance would be fixed: eyebrows plucked, teeth straightened, hair styled and advice given on clothing and makeup. An actor might be instructed to go on a diet to slim down to a size that would look good on screen; in the case of the young Judy Garland, she was told to take slimming pills containing amphetamines to bring her weight down—pills to which she became addicted. The studios chose an image and personality for each of their stars, and cast them in movies that reflected that image. Douglas Fairbanks was the swashbuckling action hero; Greta Garbo was a vamp; Claudette Colbert was a screwball comedienne; and Clark Gable was a smart-talking womanizer. For an actor to change genres or play against type might alienate the moviegoing fans, so it hardly ever happened.

EARLY '20S SCANDALS

Oversized comedy actor Fatty Arbuckle threw a raucous two-day party in a hotel in September 1921, and one of the guests was a thirty-year-old actress named Virginia Rappe. She fell ill at the party and later died of acute peritonitis and a ruptured bladder. A friend of hers claimed Fatty had raped and assaulted her, causing her death; it took three trials over the next six months before he was completely exonerated. But the hysterical press coverage meant that his reputation and his career were irrevocably damaged. Actress Mabel Normand was a cocaine addict, and this may have led in 1922 to the murder of her lover, Paramount director William Desmond Taylor, by a disgruntled drug dealer. And when director Thomas Ince collapsed on the yacht belonging to newspaper magnate William Randolph Hearst and later died, a rumor spread that Hearst had shot him, mistaking him for Charlie Chaplin whom he suspected of having an affair with his own mistress, Marion Davies. In fact, Ince's doctor claimed he died of a heart attack, but that never stopped the gossipmongers.

LEFT
In 1921, Fatty Arbuckle was the highest-paid actor in Hollywood; by 1922, his career was over.

THE HAYS CODE

In 1922, the studios brought in Presbyterian elder Will H. Hays to draw up a "code of behavior" for the movies, and the subsequent list he compiled was a mixture of "Don'ts and Be Carefuls." "Don'ts" included swearing, nudity, and the depiction of drug trafficking or childbirth. Directors should be careful not to show how to commit crimes such as murder or safecracking, and should be wary of portraying prostitution, rape, or men and women in bed together. In 1934, this was tightened up into the Hays Code, with the general rule that no picture should lower the moral standards of those who watched it. There must be no drinking, crime must be punished, and sex outside marriage should never seem appealing. Films had to get a certificate before release, but filmmakers found ingenious ways to get around the Code. Alcoholics could be shown swigging from a bottle in silhouette, and a man and a woman could lie in bed together so long as one of them had a foot on the floor. By the 1950s, the Code was losing its grip in the face of competition from realist films made in other countries, and in 1967 it was replaced by a ratings system.

The studios wanted their stars' behavior off screen to mirror the on-screen image, and every actor was made to sign a morals clause, promising that they wouldn't do anything to jeopardize their reputation. Actresses couldn't leave home without being impeccably dressed and wearing full makeup, while actors must always behave like gentlemen, because there were spies on every set who would gleefully report back to the gossip columnists. On the West Coast, Louella Parsons was joined by Hedda Hopper and Sheila Graham, between them forming what was known as the "unholy trinity," while in New York there lurked the notoriously unscrupulous Walter Winchell. If you valued your career, you did all you could to ingratiate yourself with these powerful characters, because they could

© UNDERWOOD & UNDERWOOD
STUDIO, WASHINGTON

make or break an actor with a few lines of type. They didn't need facts; insinuation and innuendo would do.

With so much at stake, you might have thought actors would tread carefully—but they rarely did. Hardly any of the stars from the Golden Age of Hollywood married and stayed faithful to the same person for life. Temptation was all around and, in some cases, it seems actors fell for the glamorous character their costar was playing onscreen; the reality check came all too soon when there wasn't a scriptwriter around to write the offset dialogue. At a time when production codes (like the 1934 Hays Code) were calling for Christian moral values to be reflected in movies, there were steamy extramarital affairs being conducted on virtually every film set.

With so much at stake, you might have thought actors would tread carefully——but they rarely did

FIREFIGHTING

Actors having extramarital sex was not the only problem faced by harassed studio bosses. There were a number of homosexual actors, and their secret leaking out could ruin careers overnight in an era when sodomy was illegal. The profession also seemed to attract a higher-than-average percentage of folk with drink problems, despite the fact that the sale of alcohol was illegal during the Prohibition era from 1920 to 1933. To counter this and other troubling behavior by the stars, studios pursued a two-pronged approach.

First of all, during the heyday of the studio system between the 1920s and the 1940s, stars could be punished for transgressions. Their wages could be docked or, worse still, they could be denied the opportunity to act in the best films. According to their contracts they were obliged to make a certain number of movies a year, and if they misbehaved they might find they were offered only mediocre scripts or else loaned out to other studios to work on *their* mediocre scripts. Actors didn't like being loaned out because they were not treated with the same respect by other studios.

The second reaction to scandal was firefighting by studio publicists. These hardy souls made friends in high places so that they could bribe police officers and district attorneys not to charge stars with felonies such as drunk driving or carelessly discharging firearms (as Ava Gardner and Frank Sinatra did in 1949 when they shot out the streetlights in the town of Indio, near Palm Springs). Publicists also carefully cultivated their relationships with the gossip columnists so that if one of them

OPPOSITE
Will Hays, who was brought in to clean up the movie industry. Producers were supposed to clear their scripts with his office before the cameras started to roll.

Rock Hudson was accompanied to the premiere of Giant *on October 10, 1956, by his wife, Phyllis Gates. She claimed she hadn't known he was gay when they married, but left him in 1957 after he had an affair with a man.*

caught a whiff of scandal, she could be persuaded not to write about it—either by the offer of an exclusive on some other story or by the threat of access to the studio's other stars being withheld. In 1955, when *Confidential* magazine was about to run a story that Rock Hudson was gay, his agent stalled them by offering scoops on two of his other clients, then quickly married Rock to his secretary Phyllis Gates. The marriage didn't last and his homosexuality remained an open secret in Hollywood, but it was not widely published in the media until after his death from AIDS in 1985. In 1948, when Robert Mitchum was caught smoking marijuana in the apartment of a young actress who was not his wife, it could have ended his career. Instead, the studio stuck by him after he apologized, served a brief prison term, then was reunited with his wife and family. It helped that he normally played a shady antihero in his movies rather than a squeaky-clean family man. It was harder to protect Ingrid Bergman when she left her husband having recently played a nun. Normally, the more famous stars would be rescued and rehabilitated, but numerous lesser names were dumped by the wayside for their transgressions and never heard of again.

THE TRUTH BEHIND
ON-SCREEN ROMANCES

It Happened One Night (1934) is a compelling comedy starring Claudette Colbert as a spoiled high-society girl who falls in love with Clark Gable's roguish reporter. Their chemistry is very romantic, but in fact Colbert was one of the only costars Gable never succeeded in getting into bed. When Paul Henreid lit two cigarettes and gave one to Bette Davis in *Now, Voyager* (1942), it was a classic moment in movie romance, but there was no spark between the two actors; she had tried to block his casting thinking he looked like a "slicked-back gigolo." Spencer Tracy and Katharine Hepburn appeared in nine battle-of-the-sexes movies together, but the public had no idea till after his death that there had been anything more than screen kisses between them. When they made *Casablanca* (1942), Ingrid Bergman and Humphrey Bogart were both firmly ensconced with other lovers, as were Vivien Leigh and Clark Gable during *Gone With the Wind* (1939). But there are plenty of romantic movies that did mark the start of a romance between its costars; for example, when Paul Newman's drifter seduced Joanne Woodward's schoolteacher in *The Long Hot Summer* (1958), it was the beginning of a love affair that lasted till his death in 2008.

LEFT
*Clark Gable and
Claudette Colbert in
It Happened One Night
(1934). They were friends
on the set but that was all.*

THE STARS FIGHT BACK

After World War II, the Hollywood studio system began to fall apart. An antimonopoly suit called the Paramount Decrees (1948) meant that studios could no longer own the distribution arm of the business but would have to deal with independent distributors. This meant they couldn't guarantee showings for the kind of "filler" movies they had often produced to keep their actors in work. Fewer movies would mean smaller stables of stars and a lot of actors would find themselves out of work.

Next, the Cold War spawned an atmosphere of hysteria as everyone began looking for "Reds under the bed." Senator Joe McCarthy launched a witch-hunt at the House Committee on Un-American Activities hearings, and set his sights on Hollywood in particular. Some right-wingers, such as Walt Disney and Louis B. Mayer, happily cooperated, but a group of screenwriters and directors known as the Hollywood Ten were jailed for being Communist sympathizers, and hundreds more were blacklisted. Charlie Chaplin, Dolores del Rio, and Paul Robeson were the best-known actors who found themselves out of a job. And while the studios were still reeling from the paranoia engendered by the HUAC, along came television to take away their audiences. Why go out to a theater when you can watch movies from the comfort of your own home?

BELOW
The Hollywood Ten, with their attorneys, leaving a House Committee on Un-American Activities hearing. All ten were cited for contempt because they refused to answer questions about their links with communism. They were each sentenced to between six and twelve months in prison, as well as being blacklisted.

At the same time, actors were beginning to rebel against the shackles of their studio system contracts. Back in 1936 when Bette Davis became disillusioned with the scripts being offered by Warner Brothers, she left to find work in England. The studio couldn't be seen to allow dissension in the ranks so they sued and forced her to return. However, in 1944 Olivia de Havilland won an important legal ruling against Warner Brothers that freed her from her contract with them. During the 1950s, more stars turned their backs on the studios and struck out alone. It meant they didn't have guaranteed work or a weekly salary but they preferred the freedom to choose their own scripts. New talent agencies sprang up and the balance of power tilted from the studios to the stars and their high-powered agents, like the legendary Lew Wasserman. It was the scenario the studios had always feared: actors began making stratospheric demands, wanting both an upfront fee and a percentage of the box-office receipts. Cary Grant commanded 10 percent of the gross for *To Catch a Thief* (1955), amounting to $700,000. And Elizabeth Taylor was the first actor to get

ABOVE
Bette Davis in crime drama Marked Woman *(1937), the first movie she made after being forced by Warner Brothers to return to Hollywood. It had a good script and helped to establish her as a star.*

ABOVE
Cary Grant plays a retired jewel thief in Hitchcock's To Catch a Thief *(1955). During filming his costar Grace Kelly caught a prince, after being introduced to Prince Rainier of Monaco, whom she would marry in 1956.*

a million-dollar fee when cast as the lead in *Cleopatra* (1963). She eventually took home $7 million after negotiating overtime payments and forcing the studio to use film stock to which she owned the rights.

The downside of leaving the studios was that actors were out on a limb when it came to dealing with scandal, as Elizabeth Taylor discovered when she had an affair with Richard Burton, her *Cleopatra* costar. She had alienated the gossip columnists by refusing them interviews and suddenly found herself isolated when a media furor erupted. Far from protecting her, Twentieth Century Fox sued her and Burton for bringing the film into disrepute, a case that was settled out of court. In subsequent decades, stars would hire their own publicists to protect their media images, but married actors having affairs with each other would continue to generate fevered headlines. Kristen Stewart's much-discussed admission of a fling with a married director in 2012, behind the back of her *Twilight* costar and lover Robert Pattinson, proved the appetite for such stories has not grown any less over the fifty years since Burton and Taylor first kissed off set.

FINDING TRUE LOVE IN HOLLYWOOD

The Hollywood couples whose romances stood the test of time were the ones who were able to find privacy, a space in which to discover if they had anything in common after the director called "Cut!" They were the ones who could hold off the pressure to wed in haste that came from the gossip industry and the studios. After a decent length of courtship they slipped away to marry in secret, thus preventing the wedding from becoming a media circus. And they endeavored to avoid long separations when each was on a different movie set on other sides of the world.

Often, this meant the woman stepping back to let her man have the limelight—but she would still be well advised to go on location with him (as Lauren Bacall did on *The African Queen*, for example). Movie folk all know what happens on movie sets, and it makes them suspicious partners. Finally, many movie marriages stood the test of time because one partner turned a blind eye to infidelity. It can simply be par for the course in an industry where a star's value is often determined by their sex appeal.

Movie stars may have more money than most, but they have a tougher time when it comes to finding true love. This book is a celebration of some who did experience the real thing—for a while at least.

Movie stars may have more money than most, but they have a tougher time when it comes to finding true love

DOUGLAS FAIRBANKS

&

MARY PICKFORD

DOUGLAS ELTON THOMAS ULLMAN

BORN: MAY 23, 1883
DENVER, COLORADO

DIED: DECEMBER 12, 1939
SANTA MONICA, CALIFORNIA

GLADYS MARIE SMITH

BORN: APRIL 8, 1892
TORONTO, CANADA

DIED: MAY 29, 1979
SANTA MONICA, CALIFORNIA

★

MARRIED: MARCH 28, 1920
BEVERLY HILLS, CALIFORNIA

OPPOSITE
Together at last after all the heartache—Mary and Douglas on their honeymoon aboard SS Lapland, June 1920.

Swashbuckling star Douglas Fairbanks literally swept America's sweetheart Mary Pickford off her feet. While on a hike with friends, they had to cross a river via stepping stones. She hesitated in her high heels, and he leaped to her aid, gallantly lifting her to safety while her then-husband stood watching.

*B*oth Douglas and Mary came from poor backgrounds, both were abandoned at the age of five by their alcoholic fathers, both struggled hard to build their careers, and both were astute in business. They had many things in common, but they were also very different people.

Mary was born Gladys Marie Smith, the eldest of three children of a Toronto couple. When she was five, her father walked out and when she was six, he died as the result of an accident on the paddle steamer where he worked. Her mother, Charlotte, struggled to raise the family and briefly considered letting a well-off local couple adopt Gladys, but the young girl refused to go when she heard that the rest of the family couldn't come too. She and her mother became inseparable, and when Charlotte came up with the idea of putting the children on stage when a local theater offered eight dollars a week for child actors, Gladys enthusiastically agreed.

At the age of seven she made her stage debut in a Victorian melodrama called *The Silver King*, and found she loved acting. Charlotte entered all three children into a string of touring productions, and for the next seven years they traveled from one shabby boarding house to the next, playing in third-rate theaters. During this period, Gladys learned negotiating skills by watching her mother haggling over every last cent.

In 1907, when Gladys was fifteen, she bravely marched into the office of leading New York impresario David Belasco and talked him into giving her work. He liked her pluck, and her pretty face framed in long blonde ringlets, but suggested she change her name to the more stylish

OPPOSITE
One of Mary's earliest reviews described her as "a flash of sunlight across a dark room, a white moth glimmering in the dusk." She described the brave, dashing Douglas (below), who once did a handstand on the rim of the Grand Canyon, as "the personification of the new world."

Mary Pickford, before giving her a Broadway debut in *The Warrens of Virginia*. Still there were periods without work, so Charlotte told Mary to visit the Biograph studios where innovative movie director D. W. Griffith was working. "The thing that most attracted me was the intelligence that shone from her face," he later recalled. Mary quickly realized that movies required a different style of acting from theater, with more subtle, natural expressions and gestures. Soon she was playing major roles in Griffith's movies, and had negotiated for herself a fee of ten dollars a day—double the going rate.

Charlotte did not approve when Mary fell in love with another Biograph actor, the Irish-born Owen Moore. She banned him from the house, but this only served to drive Mary into his arms. They eloped and got married in 1911, only telling Charlotte about it several months later. Some biographers think that Mary became pregnant and had an illegal abortion around this time, an operation that rendered her incapable of further pregnancies. The marriage was soon in trouble. Owen was a drinker, like Mary's father, and he became abusive and violent when drunk. His career was on the slide but Mary's was ascending; she signed a movie contract with Adolph Zukor of the Famous Players Lasky studio, and her reputation grew with every movie she made. She played the kind of girl American women wanted to be, and the one men wanted to marry: sweet and innocent but tough at the same time.

Then, in 1915 at a salon in New York, Mary met Douglas Fairbanks. He came over to express his admiration for her acting but she wasn't immediately impressed. "I thought he was too exuberant," she later explained in her autobiography. "I was intolerant, maybe, and not in a happy mood that day." She had no inkling that just a few months later she would begin to see him in an entirely new light.

A MAN OF ACTION

After Douglas's Jewish father walked out on the family, his mother gave him and his brothers the surname Fairbanks, after her first husband, the one with whom she had been happiest. Little Doug drove her crazy as a youngster, perpetually active, always pulling crazy stunts:

> *"I thought he was too exuberant... I was intolerant, maybe, and not in a happy mood that day"*

ABOVE
"Luminous tenderness in a steel band of gutter ferocity," said Photoplay magazine of Mary in 1916. She might look sweet, but there was no one tougher when it came to contract negotiations.

OPPOSITE
The Hollywoodland sign became a symbol of the movie capital. In 1949 the Los Angeles council voted to remove "land."

doing gymnastics, taking wild leaps from high walls, and exuding sheer boyish exuberance. He channeled his energy into acting, taking parts both in school productions and in summertime shows at Denver's Elitch Gardens Theatre. His love of pranks often got him into trouble, even prompting one school to ask him to leave after he dressed up all the statues on the school grounds. At the age of seventeen he moved to New York to join a Shakespearean acting troupe, at the instigation of Frederick Barkham Warde, a notable English actor who noticed him while on tour in Denver. This didn't pay him enough to live on, so Douglas also took odd jobs in a hardware store and as a clerk, and gradually began to build his career on Broadway, where his athleticism and dark-skinned, Hispanic looks made him natural leading-man material.

In 1907, he married an heiress named Beth Sully, and together they had a son, Douglas Fairbanks, Jr. Her father tried to persuade Doug, Sr. to get a proper job so he could keep his daughter in the style to which she was accustomed, but he had caught the

EARLY HOLLYWOOD

In the late 19th century, the area now known as Hollywood was agricultural land 10 miles east of Los Angeles, where oranges, lemons, grapes, and barley were grown. A real-estate developer called H. C. Whitley had the foresight to buy up some plots of land in the mid-1880s, and he subsequently paid to bring electricity to the area. In 1910, the community voted to merge with Los Angeles to take advantage of their water and sewage systems. The Nestor Film Company of New Jersey saw the potential of this area, with its year-round sunshine, and began producing pictures there. D. W. Griffith became the first major director to work in Hollywood. He made *In Old California* in 1910 and the film studios quickly followed. Soon the big five—Famous Players Lasky (now Paramount), Louis B. Mayer Pictures (now MGM), Warner Brothers, Radio Pictures, Inc. (RKO), and Fox—had studios in Hollywood, and a string of swanky bars and hotels sprang up to serve the actors and actresses who flocked to the area. In 1923, the iconic "Hollywoodland" sign was first erected as an advertising billboard, and became a symbol of movie glamor.

acting bug, and this put a strain on the marriage. In 1915 Doug got
his first role in a D. W. Griffith movie, *The Lamb*. More roles followed
through which he secured his reputation as the original action hero:
someone who could leap on and off horses, rescue maidens in distress,
win any sword fight, and make audiences laugh at the same time.
His popularity grew—when he started saying "Gee whiz!" the nation
followed, while the badminton-like ball game he invented, called
"Doug," was soon taken up across the country. He had a sunny
personality both on and off stage, and was a bon viveur who liked
nothing more than being surrounded by dozens of friends.

Doug's social circle had begun to overlap with that of Mary and
Owen, and one night in 1915 he witnessed Owen being rude to her.
He approached her later, they ended up dancing together, and a
flame was lit. They began to meet secretly and had soon fallen for
one another. They became closer still in late 1916 after his mother died.
The pair went for a drive in Central Park and, overcome with emotion,
he stopped the car, leaned on the wheel, and sobbed. Mary comforted
him and, when he'd composed himself again, they noticed that the
dashboard clock had stopped. They decided it meant that his mother
was watching and approved of the match, and from then on they talked
about their love being "by the clock." In 1917 they toured the country
selling Liberty Bonds to support America's involvement in World War I,
overjoyed to be able to spend so much time together. But what could
they do? Divorce would create a huge scandal, and they worried it
would ruin both their careers just at the point when they were reaching
the heights of their fame.

UNITED AT LAST

When Mary's contract with Zukor came up for negotiation in 1916,
she convinced him to agree to her having her own production company,
in which she had a share in the creative control with Zukor's people.
In 1917 Douglas also set up his own company, Douglas Fairbanks Film
Corporation. Zukor did all he could to keep Mary under contract to
his Famous Players Lasky, but in 1919 she left for another studio, First
National. Zukor then schemed to merge the two companies, a move
which would have given him power over the salaries of all creative
personnel as well as the distribution of all movies. Alarmed, Mary and
Douglas, together with Douglas's good friend Charlie Chaplin and the
director D. W. Griffith, founded their own studio, United Artists, in
order to have control over the pictures they made. One industry

observer commented, "The lunatics are taking over the asylum," and few thought they would succeed, but they were reckoning without the business acumen of Mary and Douglas. Chaplin was astonished by Mary: "She knew all the nomenclature, the amortizations, the deferred stocks. She understood all the articles of incorporation," he recalled. They had to fight Zukor's stranglehold over the country's movie theaters but were also prepared to pay top dollar for the best talent and slowly they built a stable of artists that included Gloria Swanson and Buster Keaton.

Meanwhile, Mary and Douglas were falling deeper and deeper in love. When Beth finally found out about the affair in 1919, she was shocked, as she had considered Mary a friend of hers as well as her husband's, but she agreed to give Douglas a divorce in return for a settlement of half a million dollars. Mary hesitated, near breaking point with the strain. Owen pleaded with her not to leave him and at the same time threatened to kill Douglas. Her mother's advice was to follow her heart, and when Douglas gave her an ultimatum—"Marry me or it's over"—she knew she couldn't face losing him. In California she

ABOVE
Making movie history: D. W. Griffith, Mary Pickford, Charlie Chaplin (seated), and Douglas Fairbanks (right), with lawyers Albert Banzhaf and Dennis F. O'Brien (in the background) at the signing of the contract that established United Artists. No one expected them to succeed, but in 1955 Mary sold her share for $1.5 million.

would have had to wait a year for the divorce to go through, so she went to Nevada, where she only had to be resident for six months (a detail her lawyer fixed for her with a little light forgery). On March 2, 1920, wearing black, she was divorced from Owen in Nevada and on March 28, in white tulle trimmed with apple green, she married Douglas in Beverly Hills.

But how would the public react? Would they reject their screen idols for having the effrontery to divorce? The couple got their answer while on a honeymoon that started in New York and went from there to London to Paris. Everywhere they were mobbed. Thousands of fans waited day and night to catch a glimpse of them, throw flowers at them, and scream in adulation. At least twice they had to be rescued as the mob threatened to overwhelm them. Far from being scorned, they were now the two most famous individuals on the planet

DOUGANDMARY

As a wedding present, Douglas gave Mary a former hunting lodge in Beverly Hills, which they named Pickfair, and this was soon the venue for glittering celebrity parties and dinners. Douglas often came home from filming with an entourage of thirty or forty "buddies" he'd invited for dinner or a swim in their fabulous pond, which had its own beach.

BELOW
Douglas on the set of The Thief of Baghdad (1924), in which he battles for the hand of a beautiful princess. It was one of the most expensive movies of the 1920s, featuring a flying horse, a magic carpet, and a magnificent palace set.

He was a friend to everyone and would bring home people he met in passing: a homeless man, a professional wrestler, or extras working on his movies. The practical jokes he had loved as a boy continued, and dinner might feature rubber forks, glasses that made guests dribble when they drank from them, and an infamous chair that gave unwary users an electric shock. Douglas exercised constantly to burn off his excess energy, with horse-riding, gymnastics, and weightlifting followed by a Turkish bath. "He was a little boy, always," Mary said. "He was just in life

> *"He was just in life as he was on screen"*

he was on screen." They had pet names for each other—Hipper and Tupper, or Tiller and Duber—but to their friends they were DougandMary, an indication of their closeness.

Business was booming. *The Mark of Zorro* (1921) was a huge success for Douglas, followed by *The Three Musketeers* (also 1921), *Robin Hood* (1922), *The Thief of Baghdad* (1924), and *The Black Pirate* (1926), all of them box-office gold. Mary had hits in the 20s with *Pollyanna* (1920), *Rosita* (1923), and *My Best Girl* (1927). But in 1928, the couple's luck began to change. Mary's mother died on March 21 that year, and she simply fell apart. "She was almost my very life," she wrote, and without Charlotte's advice, she wasn't sure if she could carry on. On June 21, in a deep depression, she attacked her famous head of hair with a pair of scissors and cut off the long blonde ringlets that had been her trademark. Douglas burst into tears when he saw the short bob she adopted instead.

Then came the talking pictures that every silent-screen actor dreaded. Until that point, the public hadn't known what actors sounded like, and the early recording technology could make a perfectly normal voice sound laughable. Careers were suddenly on the line. In addition, Douglas was still playing roles in which he was the ever-young action hero, leaping onto mantelpieces in the midst of a swordfight or jumping from airplanes, feats which for a man now over the age of forty had become a stretch. And Douglas was so annoyed when costar Buddy Rogers flirted with Mary on the set of *My Best Girl* that he had a brief affair with an actress named Lupe Vélez on *The Gaucho*, the first infidelity to mar the perfect relationship. Mary and Douglas decided to make a talkie together in 1929, and chose *The Taming of the Shrew*, the Shakespearean tale of marital strife, but the shoot was troubled. Douglas often turned up late on set, without having learned his lines, and the couple argued publicly. Everyone could see the cracks appearing.

ABOVE
On the beach with a movie camera (top) and playing a street singer in Rosita (1923). During her career Mary got involved in all aspects of making movies, from acting and producing to distribution.

ABOVE
"DougandMary" in a canoe in the swimming pool at Pickfair. They threw legendary parties at the house, with guests including Albert Einstein, George Bernard Shaw, Amelia Earhart, President Franklin D. Roosevelt and his wife Eleanor, and a host of movie stars.

"When a man finds himself sliding downhill, he should do everything to reach bottom in a hurry and pass out of the picture," Fairbanks announced, and he took up world travel as a substitute for filmmaking. He went to China, Mongolia, the Philippines, Suez, Morocco, and all over Europe. Mary accompanied him on some of his trips, but by 1931 she was running out of patience: "I just couldn't keep up the pace with a man whose very being had become motion, no matter how purposeless." During 1931, the inevitable happened when Douglas met English socialite Lady Sylvia Ashley at a party in London. She was a model and dancer, married to a lord; she was also twenty-six to his forty-eight. Mary heard rumors of his infidelity, and turned for comfort to Buddy Rogers. Neither wanted to let go of their marriage and things were on again/off again for a while, until one day Douglas sent her a telegram saying he would not be returning. Mary showed it to gossip columnist Louella Parsons, aware that doing so meant the story would run in the papers. But it was time for a decision one way or the other and finally, in January 1936, they were divorced.

Neither Douglas nor Mary really wanted a divorce. They still loved each other but could not see a way forward. Mary went on to marry Buddy Rogers, and to adopt two children with him. Douglas married Sylvia, but they didn't have long together before he died of a heart attack in 1939, at the age of fifty-six. Near the end, he asked one of his brothers to give a message to Mary: "By the clock." The meaning was clear; he had never stopped loving her. Mary was so upset she could not bring herself to attend the funeral, and the alcoholism that ran in the family began to take hold of her. Her later years were overshadowed by depression and she became a virtual recluse in Pickfair, refusing to come out from behind its walls. Old friends who tried to visit were put off by Buddy and rarely saw her. Perhaps it is true that in every life there is only room for one great love. Mary had hers, lost it, and knew she would never find its like again.

ACADEMY AWARDS

Douglas Fairbanks was the first president of the Academy of Motion Picture Arts and Sciences, an organization that was the brainchild of Louis B. Mayer. Fairbanks hosted their first-ever awards ceremony, on May 16, 1929, at the Hollywood Roosevelt Hotel. Tickets to the dinner cost five dollars, and the ceremony itself lasted just fifteen minutes, during which awards were presented in twelve categories. Emil Jannings received Best Actor and Janet Gaynor took Best Actress, while Charlie Chaplin received a special award for all the work he had done on the movie *The Circus*. The following year Mary Pickford would win Best Actress for her role in *Coquette*. MGM art director Cedric Gibbons designed the statuette they were awarded, which shows a knight clutching a sword and standing on a reel of film. It weighs 8½ pounds and is 11½ inches tall. Various apocryphal tales surround the way it came to be called an "Oscar," but the best-known is that Academy librarian Margaret Herrick remarked that it resembled her Uncle Oscar, and the name stuck.

LEFT
William C. DeMille gives Mary the Best Actress Oscar for her role in My Best Girl, 1929.

RUDOLPH VALENTINO

&

NATACHA RAMBOVA

RODOLFO ALFONSO RAFFAELLO PIERRE FILIBERT GUGLIELMO DI VALENTINA D'ANTONGUOLLA	**WINIFRED KIMBALL SHAUGHNESSY**
BORN: MAY 6, 1895 CASTELLENETA, ITALY	BORN: JANUARY 19, 1897 SALT LAKE CITY, UTAH
DIED: AUGUST 23, 1926 NEW YORK CITY	DIED: JUNE 5, 1966 PASADENA, CALIFORNIA

★

MARRIED: MAY 13, 1922 AND MARCH 14, 1923
MEXICALI, MEXICO

OPPOSITE
Rudolph and Natacha dancing together, c. 1923. He was an accomplished dancer who earned his living as a paid dance-hall partner on arrival in America.

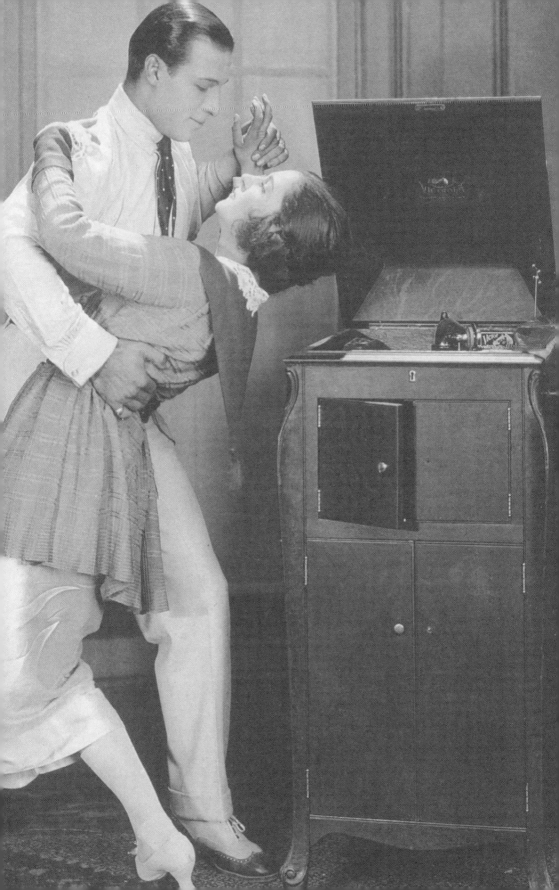

Rudolph and Natacha were hounded by press accusations that they were homosexual and their marriage was a sham, but for most of the four years they spent together, they were as close as it is possible for two people to be.

Rudolph was born in Castellaneta in southern Italy, a small town just on the instep of the Italian boot. He was a lively rebel who didn't work at school—his report cards all came back marked "*Respinte*" (failed)—but his mother could never stay mad at him for long. "He had such a beautiful face. Like a cherub," she told her neighbors. Rudolph adored his mama, who came from France and to him was the epitome of femininity: a good homemaker and a joyful spirit who loved to dance and whirl her son around the kitchen. His father was a veterinary surgeon who, while researching a cure for malaria when Rudolph was just eleven years old, accidentally caught the disease himself and died. Rudolph was always an emotional child and sobbed openly over this loss. After leaving school he was sent to a technical school in Perugia to learn about agriculture, but such a career held no appeal. He had a yearning for adventure and at the end of 1913, when he was eighteen years old, his mother paid his fare to America on the *SS Cleveland*, giving him all the money she could afford to help him make a new life.

It was snowing and just before Christmas when Rudolph arrived in New York. He had never felt so lonely (or so cold) in his life, but he managed to make some friends who introduced him to the world of the dance hall, where older women would pay ten cents for a dance with a handsome partner. He was popular there but got involved in a bit of trouble with the divorce case of one of his dance partners, so a friend suggested he try the movie business instead. He made his way to Los Angeles and began queuing daily at the studios in the hope of getting work as an extra. His first role was as a dancer in a movie called *Alimony* (1917), and more bit parts followed, but his dark looks meant he was cast as a villain rather than a leading man. Director D. W. Griffith rejected

BELOW
Rudolph was plagued by homesickness, but in his early Hollywood years he seldom had the money to sail back to Italy, and later he didn't have much spare time.

him as "too foreign-looking," adding, "The girls would never like him." Then, in 1919, word arrived that his mother had died suddenly, and Rudolph was so heartbroken he considered giving up and going back to Italy.

At this low point, Rudolph met an actress named Jean Acker, fell head over heels in love with her, and within a few weeks had persuaded her to marry him by special license. They drove to the Hollywood Hotel after the ceremony and, just as he prepared to lift her over the threshold into their room, she slammed the door in his face. He was bewildered when she yelled through the door that the marriage had been a mistake. She was a lesbian, who had been involved in a love triangle with two other women and had married to escape them, but then realized she could not be his wife. Rudolph was upset and humiliated by the fiasco. Fortunately, his career took a turn for the better around this time when a screenwriter named June Mathis took an interest in him and landed him a part in *The Four Horsemen of the Apocalypse*, the movie that would first make his name. The scene in which he dances the tango, gripping his partner tightly and ending with a passionate kiss, made female moviegoers swoon. His career was in the ascendant when, in 1921, he was introduced to Natacha Rambova, an art director who was looking for a leading man for a new movie, *Camille*. It wasn't love at first sight—not on her part anyway—but it wasn't long before they realized they were kindred spirits.

THE ICICLE MELTS

Natacha was born in Salt Lake City to an Irish immigrant father and a Mormon mother, but the marriage didn't last and her mother went on to marry three more times, moving up in the world with each one. Natacha was related via one of the marriages to the famous interior designer Elsie de Wolfe, who took her to Paris and enrolled her in ballet classes during summer vacations while she was at boarding school in England. She wanted to pursue ballet as a career and, when she was seventeen, an aunt invited her to New York, where she was accepted by the Theodore Kosloff dance company. Kosloff seduced her, gave her the Russian-sounding name by which she would come to be best known, and became a controlling influence in her life. She grew too tall to be a classical dancer but had a strong talent for design, and began sketching costumes and sets for the company, for which Kosloff took the credit. She only escaped his stranglehold when she took some costume sketches to actress Alla Nazimova, who offered to

OPPOSITE
Magazine readers lapped up stories about Rudolph and Natacha, who were seen as the epitome of glamor.

and beneath her smart, close-fitting hat her hair is braided in long, glistening coils over her ears. She is what one means when one says a woman looks "finished."

Gladys Hall and Adele Whitely Fletcher enhance the party by adding . . . numbers. They are Two More People. By no possible stretch of the imagination can we do more for them saving perhaps to note that they are clad like most of the modern young women one sees about in garments carefully selected to do service not only for luncheon parties but also for shopping orgies, for tea in the late afternoon, for dinner in the evening, for theater parties and for midnight suppers.

RODOLPH VALENTINO (*rather ruefully*): Now somebody else comes out to say that they discovered me! It is amazing! Every day some one else "discovers" me. How can so many people discover one solitary man? I could not be so variously discovered. It is not possible. Every way, every day, somebody else, they discover me! Why do they want to what you call discover me? Even your America had not so many. And the one who actually did discover me, she says nothing at all. Isn't that like this life? But when I think of some of the awful pictures I made in my "past" I wonder that anyone thinks it a credit to them.

NATACHA RAMBOVA: Rudy, I think you ought to tell definitely who did discover you. After all, you

All photographs by Abbé

"When I signed to play Julio in 'The Four Horsemen of the Apocalypse,'" explained R. Valentino, "I did nothing but read about Julio and think about Julio. I knew how Julio felt with every breath he drew. I knew him as well as I know my best friend." Above, Natacha Valentino in the costume in which she dances; and at the left, Valentino as Julio—also the costume in which he dances

ought to know. (*Her voice is the antithesis of Rudy's, being cool and clear with only now and again the deep note constantly slurring his and giving it depth and color.*)

ADELE WHITELY FLETCHER (*Always the Editor-or-die!*): That's a good idea, Mister Valentino. Why dont you tell Miss Hall and me. We'll write about it and call it "We Discover Who Discovered Valentino." It's a vicarious triumph for us, but one does what one can! We'll do one of those double interviews on it. What do you say, Gladys?

GLADYS HALL (*who has been silently thanking heaven that she at last has the opportunity of eating without questioning*): I was *told* that this was a *social* luncheon. I seem to have been misinformed. I'll do no interview. I'm an I. W. W. today. Which means, in my case, *I Wont Write!* I want my hors d'œuvres in peace and without punctuation.

RODOLPH VALENTINO (*with some of that famed gallantry that has made him "Every Husband's Rival"*): Certainly not now. Miss Hall is right. I would not hear of it. At my apartment ,whenever you say. Or, if you would prefer it, at Mrs. Valentino's apartment. You know, the courts say, they say that we are not yet married. So—we have two apartments.*

ADELE WHITELY FLETCHER (*with a despairing glance at her undiplomatic confrère*): Oh, Lord! Heaven help us that staff writers are not only inelegant but scarce! St-tt-t-tt-tt—*Gladys!*

*Courts and Cupid have now made the two apartments one!

LAVENDER MARRIAGES

During the 1920s, studios began to include morality clauses in their stars' contracts, hoping to avoid any major scandals that might affect box-office earnings. Homosexuality was a particular taboo and some stars entered into marriages of convenience, known as lavender marriages, to hide their sexual orientation from press and public. Alla Nazimova was in a lavender marriage with British actor Charles Bryant from 1912 to 1925, while continuing to pursue lesbian affairs. When it came out that the marriage had not been consummated, the gossip harmed her career. William Haines, an MGM leading man, lived with his male partner Jimmie Shields, and Joan Crawford called them "the happiest married couple in Hollywood." But his refusal to enter into a lavender marriage with a woman led to the movie roles drying up in the early 1930s. Speculation continues to this day about whether Rudolph Valentino and Natacha Rambova's marriage concealed their true sexuality, but there is no plausible evidence of either of them sleeping with a member of the same sex and plenty of evidence of their heterosexual affairs.

RIGHT
The glamorous Alla Nazimova.

help her establish a career in movies. Kosloff was so furious when she told him she was leaving that he fired a shotgun loaded with bird-shot at her, wounding her in the thigh.

Nazimova hired Natacha as an art director to work on her productions, an association that would later lead to claims that Natacha must be bisexual. Nazimova was part of what was known as "the Sewing Circle," a group of lesbian and bisexual actresses in Hollywood. Nazimova had once been a lover of Rudolph's wife, Jean Acker, but there is no evidence that Natacha was ever romantically involved with her. Natacha was probably disillusioned with men after her experiences with Kosloff, and gained the nickname "The Icicle" in Hollywood, but according to a friend of Rudolph's, there wasn't "one red-blooded male on the set who didn't fantasize about her." She was a classic beauty, with brown eyes, auburn hair, and aristocratic features.

According to Natacha's memoirs, her first impressions of Rudolph were, "Two dark slanting eyes with eyelashes and eyebrows white with mica [artificial snow]." He was filming a movie called *Uncharted Seas* and came to see her dressed head to toe in his costume of Arctic furs to audition for a role in *Camille*. He got the part, but at first Natacha found him annoying due to his habit of telling unfunny jokes in an effort to win popularity. She wrote, "When I learned to know Rudy better, I began to see, underneath all his forced happiness, the lonely and often sad young man he really was." They chatted about their memories of Italy and France, and he told her about his mother, whose death he had not yet reconciled. She watched him on set as he sat alone between takes to channel the necessary emotion and often struggled not to cry as the cameras rolled. She began inviting him for supper at her tiny bungalow on Sunset Boulevard and they soon became close. He helped her to lacquer her furniture black and red, Chinese-style, and together they prepared real Italian dinners, which often took so long they didn't finish eating till after midnight.

Neither of them had much money, but they loved animals and collected a miniature menagerie: a lion cub they called Zela (which had to be given to a trainer at four months old as it grew too big), a pet monkey, a huge gopher snake, and two Great Dane puppies. Natacha's stepfather was a perfume magnate, but she was too proud to ask him for help when cash was tight. Instead, she and Rudolph went out hunting in her car, shooting quail or rabbit, or gathering mussels at the seashore to fill their cooking pot. She realized early on that he was no good at managing money. He bought a Mercer car on an installment plan, only to have to hand it back when he couldn't keep up with the installments, even though it was already half paid off. She urged him to ask for higher fees for his movies—he was earning much less than other stars—and gradually their income began to improve. This was their happiest period as they

> *"Underneath all his forced happiness, the lonely and often sad young man he really was"*

BELOW
"Here was one who was catnip to women. Here was one who had wealth and fame. And here was one who was very unhappy," said Jack Dempsey, the boxer, who trained Rudolph for his movie fight scenes.

bought a house and planned to marry in spring 1922. He wrote to her, "You are to me the most precious jewell [sic] God ever gifted me with." They were young, beautiful, ambitious, and passionately in love.

A DOMINANT FORCE

Rudolph obtained a divorce from Jean Acker on March 4, 1922. His attorney warned him that he was legally obliged to wait a year before remarrying, but he wasn't concerned because he knew of many other couples in the same situation who had not bothered to do so. On May 13, he and Natacha traveled to Mexicali in Mexico, where they were married at the mayor's house, then held a wedding breakfast that lasted from morning through till seven in the evening, to the accompaniment of a string band. Soon after their return to the US, though, Rudolph was arrested on charges of bigamy. When the case came to trial he insisted, in the face of sarcastic questioning by the prosecuting lawyer, that the marriage had not been consummated. He was let off, but he and Natacha would have to wait until March 1923 before they could officially be wed.

BELOW
Natacha and Rudolph on their wedding day, with best man Douglas Gerrard, just outside the Mayor's house in Mexicali. Natacha wrote in her autobiography, "I shall always love the Mexican people for the happiness they gave us that day. There was nothing that was too much for them to do."

Meanwhile, Rudolph was becoming a genuine movie idol. The crazed reaction of fans who watched him in *The Sheikh* (1921), as he threw Agnes Ayres across his saddle and rode off into the desert, was such that a new word was coined to define him: heartthrob. His emotions shone out through his dark, hypnotic eyes, and women swooned at his virile forcefulness. The hysteria of fans in the street, however, alarmed him. In real life, Rudolph was a gentle man who was far from dominant, with Natacha the driving force in the relationship. She began to design his costumes for films and during shooting of *The Young Rajah* (1922) she phoned the set daily to urge her husband to insist on design and script changes. She was the one who forced him to hold out for ever-higher fees and more creative control. She didn't like the

parts the Famous Players Lasky studio
was casting him in and accused the
managers of sabotaging his career; for
them she became a complete thorn
in the side. In September 1922, at her
urging, Rudolph went on strike. The
studio countersued and when it ended
up in court, a judge decreed that he
must either work for Lasky or retire from
movies until 1924, when his contract
with them expired. Despite mounting
debts, Rudolph chose the latter course
and for the next year, he and Natacha
made money by touring America
promoting beauty products for the
Mineralva company.

In 1924, Natacha negotiated Rudolph's
return to film with a picture called
Monsieur Beaucaire, in which she was art
director. For his role as the Duke of
Chartres, she dressed her husband in
powdered wigs, silk stockings, and very
tight pants, a look that didn't go down
well with fans, who thought he appeared
effeminate. Then on *The Hooded Falcon*,
Natacha fell out with his scriptwriter friend June Mathis, and there
was a huge overspend on costumes and sets, which led to the studio
pulling the plug and Rudolph's contract being terminated. Another
studio, United Artists, indicated that it would be willing to hire him,
for good money, but only if Natacha was banned from the set. Her
reputation for interference was widespread. She told Rudolph to turn
down the offer but he decided to accept, leading to a rift in their
marriage. But this wasn't the only problem.

ABOVE
Rudolph in The Sheikh
*(1926). A journalist wrote,
"The women are all
dizzy over him. The men
have formed a secret
order (of which I am
running for president . . .)
to loathe, hate, and
despise him."*

Rudolph was a small-town Italian boy at heart, and he once wrote to
Natacha, "I admire in you those lovely qualities of femininity I admired
in my poor dear mother." However, if he wanted a clone of his mother,
he had picked the wrong girl. When he suggested they might start a
family together, she made it clear she didn't want children—"Homes and
babies are all very nice, but you can't have them and a career as well."
She was an extremely talented designer, who undertook meticulous

period research for each film and her work had a strong influence on 1920s cinema although, as had happened with Kosloff, she was not always given the credit. She certainly did not plan to stay home and wash diapers as Rudolph had hoped.

He drove her to the station on August 13, 1925, from where she was heading to New York for work. The inevitable photographers took snaps of their farewell kiss, but shortly afterward she announced their separation to the press. "We have been happy together and may be again," Rudolph told reporters. In fact, it was the last time they would ever see each other.

THE FINAL CREDITS ROLL

Soon after Natacha's departure, Rudolph had an affair with costar Vilma Banky, but another Hollywood icon also had him in her sights. Polish-born vamp Pola Negri boasted before they met, "Once Rudy has experienced my love, he will forget about all other women." They were introduced at a costume party and the affair began. But around this time, journalists were increasingly casting slurs on his masculinity. They satirized his hair, which was always slicked down with brilliantine, his dandyish clothing, and the fact that (they claimed) both of his wives had been homosexual. Then in July 1926, the *Chicago Tribune*, running an article claiming that American men were becoming more feminine, compared Valentino to the pink powder puffs that were being sold

> *"We have been happy together and may be again"*

with talcum powder in vending machines. Valentino was so incensed he challenged the article's writer to a boxing match, and then fought another journalist, Frank O'Neill, in his place. Valentino won, but still the rumors persisted, to his great irritation.

In August 1926, Rudolph suddenly collapsed with stomach pains while staying in New York. He was operated on for appendicitis and a gastric ulcer and when he came round from the anesthetic his first question was, "Did I behave like a pink powder puff or a man?" The hospital was bombarded with flowers and messages from fans, wishing him a speedy recovery. But just a few days after his surgery, it became clear Rudolph had developed an infection, and on August 23 he died. He was just thirty-one years old. Natacha was in France but she and Rudolph had been exchanging telegrams and discussing a reconciliation, so the news came as a huge shock to her. She locked herself in a room for three days, refusing to eat, while all around the

OPPOSITE
Mourners queued to see Rudolph's body, which looked like a wax dummy due to the embalming process. The funeral directors hired four actors to pretend to deliver a wreath from Italian dictator Benito Mussolini.

globe women reacted with hysterical grief. Rudolph's body was embalmed and placed in an open casket at the funeral home, and riots erupted as fans stampeded to see him. Songs were written in his honor and a mysterious woman in black brought red roses to his grave every year on the anniversary of his death; this may originally have been an old mistress, but soon became a stunt arranged as a tourist attraction.

Natacha married once more, but the marriage didn't last; instead she developed a distinguished career as an Egyptologist and a lecturer on the occult. Natacha was most important woman in Rudolph's life after his mother, and their relationship was made more difficult because of the sexism of the times, when pushy men were promoted but pushy women were ostracized. They were happiest in the early days, still struggling to put food on the table, when she became the mother figure he was searching for and he looked up to her with a respect she struggled to find elsewhere.

SPIRITUALISM

Spiritualism was wildly popular with movie people in 1920s Hollywood. Palm readers, astrologists, crystal gazers, and trance mediums plied a roaring trade among actors seeking guidance or reassurance on their next roles. June Mathis may have introduced Rudolph to spiritualism, as she had taken it up when her mother died, and he and Natacha often held séances at their Hollywood home to try to contact the dead. She would later claim that Rudolph received messages from the other side using a technique known as automatic writing, and that a book of poems he wrote entitled *Day Dreams* was dictated to him by spirit guides. His personal spirit guide was said to be an "Indian brave" called Black Feather. After Rudolph's sudden death, many people claimed to have contacted him in the spirit world. In 1927, a group of psychics set up an annual memorial service for him, claiming to see his ghost and communicate with him, but Natacha said that what she called the "Death Circus" was preventing Rudolph's spirit from moving on. Her memoir about him included a section entitled "Revelations," in which she reported conversations she'd had with his spirit since his death.

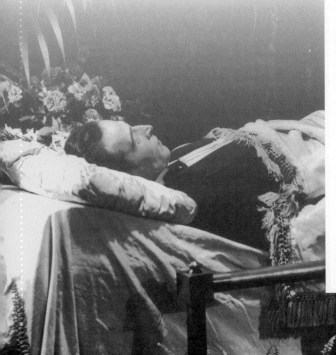

JOHN GILBERT
&
GRETA GARBO

JOHN CECIL PRINGLE

BORN: JULY 10, 1897
LOGAN, UTAH

DIED: JANUARY 9, 1936
LOS ANGELES, CALIFORNIA

GRETA LOVISA GUSTAFSSON

BORN: SEPTEMBER 18, 1905
STOCKHOLM, SWEDEN

DIED: APRIL 15, 1990
NEW YORK CITY

OPPOSITE
Greta and John in
A Woman of Affairs
(1928). Gossips
speculated about
whether she preferred
her real-life affairs
to be with men or
with women.

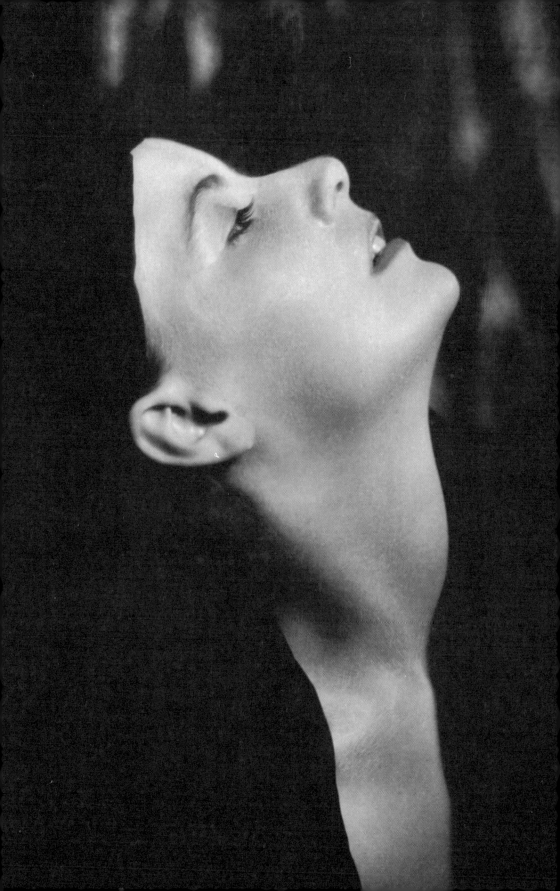

Those who witnessed John Gilbert and Greta Garbo's first screen kiss during filming of *Flesh and the Devil* spoke of seeing an "instant spark, a flash" between them, and moviegoers loved the palpable onscreen chemistry. The Swedish ice queen with America's great loverboy was a match that seemed too good to be true.

oth Greta and John were complicated characters who came from impoverished backgrounds. Greta's father was a farmworker in Södermalm, an island near Stockholm, and her mother did cleaning work to help with household expenses. They lived in a rundown three-room apartment where Greta, her two siblings, and both parents slept in the same room. When there was no money because her father was ill and couldn't work, Greta would go to a local soup kitchen and entertain the waiting lines with a little street cabaret while waiting for a meal. John's childhood wasn't quite so poverty-stricken, but his parents worked for traveling theater troupes in the American Midwest, and—especially after his father had left before the boy was ten—they were dependent on the earnings: "When we had good seasons we stayed at the best hotel and swanked it. When it was a poor one, we migrated to the cheap and nasty sections of towns," he told an *LA Times* reporter in 1922. His mother got remarried to a man named Walter Gilbert and John took his surname, but after she died when he was sixteen, he was on his own in the world. That both John and Greta reached the pinnacle of Hollywood stardom from such lowly beginnings speaks volumes about their grit and determination, as well as their talent.

Greta left school early and took a job at Stockholm's Paul Urbanus Bergström department store. While there she was invited to model hats for their spring 1921 catalog and found she enjoyed being in front of the camera. The sixteen-year-old heard that movie director Mauritz Stiller

OPPOSITE
Actress Eleanor Boardman said of her, "You can't pigeonhole Garbo. She was fascinating. Extremely selfish. Beautiful. Strange."

BELOW
A 1927 magazine story using stills from Flesh and the Devil. *Neither John nor Greta would tell the media that they were having an affair.*

was looking for young actresses and accosted him outside his house, almost causing him to crash his car. He told her to come back when she was older, so to gain experience she took part in a promotional film for the Bergström store, then got a small role in a movie comedy, after which she won a place at Stockholm's Royal Dramatic Theater Acting School. She dated a couple of boys at this time, but her first serious love affair was with a Jewish girl named Mimi Pollock, to whom she wrote passionate love letters: "The letter from you has aroused a storm of longing in me . . . I have always thought that you and I belonged together." Swedish society was more liberal than America would prove to be, and although Greta was discreet about her relationships with women, they were not something of which she was ashamed.

Stardom arrived suddenly. In 1924 she auditioned for a role in the new Mauritz Stiller movie, *The Saga of Gösta Berling*, and got the part (he didn't seem to remember their earlier meeting). Louis B. Mayer of MGM studios saw the film while in Europe and came to Stockholm to take Greta and Mauritz to dinner, where he offered each of them a contract. According to his daughter, it was Greta in whom he was more interested. She had a limited mastery of English and couldn't read

BELOW
*Greta crossing
the Atlantic with
Mauritz Stiller on
SS Drottningholm.
They arrived in New
York on July 6, 1925.
"I have to thank Mauritz
Stiller for everything in
this world," she said.*

the contract, so she asked Mauritz if she should sign and when he said yes, she scribbled her name on the page. At the end of June 1925, at just nineteen years old, she set sail for America, seemingly unaware that she had actually signed a five-year contract, because she told her mother she would be back within a year.

ADDICTED TO LOVE

Greta didn't take to America. She hated the heat of the New York summer, and the five-day train journey to Hollywood bored her senseless. She rented a tiny apartment in the Miramar Hotel on Wilshire Boulevard and spent her twentieth birthday alone in her room. Before he would put her in a movie, MGM director Irving Thalberg ordered her to go on a strict diet, have her teeth straightened, and her hair defrizzed, then he sent her out shopping with a stylist to find clothes that, as he said, didn't make her look like "a farmer's wife." The only bright spots in those early days were two important relationships she formed: one with a translator named Sven Hugo Borg, who became a close friend and personal assistant for the next four years, and the other with William Daniels, a cameraman who would light her in nineteen of her twenty-four movies and make her look so luminous on screen that she trusted him above all others.

ABOVE
Greta in The Saga of Gösta Berling *(1924), in which she had to perform her own stunts on a speeding sleigh. It was her breakout role, the one that got her noticed.*

In April 1926 Greta became distraught at the news that her sister Alva had died of tuberculosis. She was also unhappy that Stiller was replaced as director on her movie *The Temptress* after falling out with the studio (he would return to Sweden the following year). She seriously considered throwing in the towel and going home to be with her family. But MGM wanted her to make a movie called *Flesh and the Devil* with John Gilbert, who was then Hollywood's most bankable star, and she agreed, grudgingly. She didn't like the fact that she kept being cast as a vamp and was still depressed about her sister's death when she first met John on August 17. "Hi, Greta," he called out cheerily across the lot. "It's *Miss* Garbo," she replied frostily. But John's gregarious personality and his ardent screen kiss would soon melt some of that icy exterior.

> "*In front of the camera their love-making was so intense that it surpassed anything anyone had seen*"

John's route to the top had been more conventional than Greta's. After his mother died in 1913, he got work as a copy boy at a newspaper, then as a theatrical stage manager. His stepfather wrote to Thomas Ince at the Triangle Film Corporation, and Ince helped John climb the first step on the Hollywood ladder. John worked as an extra in a few movies, then in 1916 came his first sizable role with *The Apostle of Vengeance*. With each subsequent movie his billing increased, and national acclaim followed after he starred with Mary Pickford in *Heart o' the Hills* in 1919. He moved to Fox Studios to play the Count in *Monte Cristo* (1922), then to MGM for *The Big Parade* and *The Merry Widow* (both 1925). He wasn't classically good-looking but he did have a naughty-boy charisma on screen that audiences loved, and he became known as "The Great Lover"— an irony that may not have been lost on him since his personal life was in fact disastrous. Perhaps an amateur psychologist would say he was seeking a mother replacement, but he fell in love with all his leading ladies almost as soon as the cameras started rolling. The relationships never lasted because the women threw him out before long, fed up with his infidelities and heavy drinking, but there was always the next movie to look forward to, and the next ingénue.

In 1918 he married Olivia Burwell, a Southern belle whose parents had moved out to California, but she returned to Mississippi the following year. In 1922 he married actress Leatrice Joy but was never faithful to her, having affairs with costars Barbara La Marr and Laurette Taylor, among a host of others. He was desperate to attract the right woman and falling in love was almost a compulsion. It's no surprise, then, that he fell in love so fast and so hard with Greta Garbo, the stunning new girl in town. According to director Clarence Brown, "In front of the camera their lovemaking was so intense that it surpassed anything anyone had seen and made the technical staff feel their mere presence an indiscretion." For Greta, he appeared as a savior at one of the lowest points of her life and, two nights after their first screen kiss, she moved into his large Spanish-style home in the Hollywood Hills.

RAPID BURNOUT

John was dazzled by Greta, the Scandinavian beauty with the deep husky voice and the unfathomable nature. He described her as "marvelous, the most alluring creature you have ever seen. Capricious as the devil, whimsical, temperamental, and fascinating." She was homesick for Sweden so he spent $15,000 converting his bathroom into a marble and gold Scandinavian-style bathroom, and he also built a log cabin in the grounds surrounded by pine trees, installing a waterfall nearby. He bought a two-masted schooner and planned that they would spend a year cruising the South Seas on their honeymoon. And right from the start, he asked Greta to marry him, over and over again—but every time she told him no.

They shared the house with a scriptwriter named Carey Wilson, and Greta liked nothing better than to be one of the boys, hiking with them in the hills or smoking a pipe by the swimming pool. She called John "Yacky" and he called her "Flecka" (the Swedish word for woman). John threw regular Sunday parties

PROHIBITION & HOLLYWOOD

On January 16, 1920, the National Prohibition Act came into force, banning any drinks with an alcohol content of more than 3.2 percent. Total alcohol consumption across the US halved between 1920 and the repeal of the law in 1933, but many people disregarded Prohibition. Illegal bars known as speakeasies sprang up across America as alcohol was supplied by bootleggers. At first, many in Hollywood supported the ban, thinking it would make people go to the movies more, but that didn't prove to be the case. Production codes banned directors from showing the consumption of alcohol on screen, but they got around this by having actors drink with their backs to the camera or simply hold a bottle while acting drunk. Gangsters became a popular Hollywood subject, starting with *Little Caesar* in 1931.

for his many friends in the movie industry while Greta, who didn't like to socialize with strangers, would sometimes join them but more often not. She startled his guests by stripping naked to swim in the pool, not for the sake of titillation but because that's the way she had always done things back home. John and Greta rarely went out in public together, but there is an oft-repeated tale of a dinner party at which John asked her to marry him in a double wedding with director King Vidor and actress Eleanor Boardman on September 8, 1926—and this time she apparently said yes. However, on the day, according to the story, she didn't show up and John got so drunk that he punched Louis B. Mayer and knocked him to the ground. Eleanor Boardman herself is the source of this anecdote, but most biographers believe that Greta never agreed to marry John—certainly that's what she always claimed— and are skeptical that he could have knocked over the stocky MGM studio mogul. The only elements of the story that seem plausible are that Greta didn't show up and John got very drunk.

From soon after her arrival in Hollywood, Greta had refused to do interviews with reporters, despite being obliged to by her contract. She

LOUELLA PARSONS & HEDDA HOPPER

Louella Parsons was the original "Queen of Hollywood Gossip," with her *Los Angeles Examiner* column on the lives and loves of the stars syndicated to newspapers the world over and said to have 20 million readers. She could make or break a career with a few deft lines and prided herself on knowing everyone's business. If there was no news, she was happy to make it up, as she often did about Garbo and Gilbert, claiming for example that they had married on Valentine's Day 1927 and frequently putting words in their mouths.

Her articles would mysteriously quote "a friend of the star," and she had several sources on movie sets, one of whom was a character actress called Hedda Hopper. By the 1930s studio boss Louis B. Mayer considered that Parsons's influence was becoming too great, so he sponsored Hedda to create a rival column for the *LA Times*, not realizing that in doing so he was creating an even greater monster. The two women began a notorious feud, with Hedda soon showing that she was by far the bitchier and more destructive of the two.

LEFT
Hedda Hopper was sometimes attacked by angry stars. Spencer Tracy kicked her backside and Joseph Cotton pulled a chair from under her.

was an intensely private person and would cut ties with any friend who spoke to the press about her, so there are very few ways of telling her real feelings about John. She told a Swedish journalist in 1930, "He is quite a wonderful man—vital, eager, enthusiastic. If he had not come into my life at this time, I should probably have come home to Sweden at once." Her cool reserve must have driven a passionate man like John crazy. Once, during an argument when he was drunk, he pushed her off his balcony and she rolled down the hillside. As he watched, she simply picked herself up, climbed back over the rocks, and hauled herself up again without a word. At other times when he was drunk, she went back to the Miramar, where she had never given up her apartment.

Desperate to provoke a jealous reaction, John began to taunt her that he was going out to sleep with other women—either prostitutes or one of his costars—and she simply replied, "Fine, I'll leave the door open." No matter what he tried, he couldn't crack her stony self-sufficiency and his efforts only made her back away. She didn't need

ABOVE
No one knew the truth about Greta and John's relationship because they weren't saying, but it didn't stop magazines from devoting many speculative column inches to the subject.

him. She didn't appear to need anyone. Greta had been fiercely independent since childhood and she wasn't about to change.

John wasn't the only one who found her impossible to pin down. After the filming of *Flesh and the Devil*, she disappeared from sight and refused every film role MGM offered her, in breach of her contract. Furious, Louis B. Mayer threatened to have her fired and deported, and she retorted that she would simply marry Mr. Gilbert in order to get American residency and would go to work for another studio. She didn't care much about her career and that made it a nightmare to negotiate with her. Some biographers speculate that she was pregnant and had a termination during what amounted to almost 250 days of absence from her contractual obligations during 1926–27, but there is no reason to disbelieve the excuse she gave that she was suffering from anemia. Gossip columnist Louella Parsons was desperate for a scoop on the Gilbert/Garbo relationship, especially after he was seen entering the hospital in February 1927 (possibly in an attempt to dry out). But no one knows for sure what was going on.

The couple began filming *Anna Karenina* (retitled *Love*) in spring 1927, with Greta in the title role and John as Vronsky. "Garbo and Gilbert . . . in Love" read the posters, but on set they were barely talking to each other. She was still living in his house, but John was back to his old tricks of sleeping with his leading ladies. "Love comes, love goes. Who can help it?" Greta is alleged to have told a reporter, in classic enigmatic fashion.

> *"Love comes, love goes. Who can help it?"*

STILL SEARCHING

It is often claimed that the coming of the talkies ruined John Gilbert's career, but reviews of his first talking picture, *His Glorious Night* (1929), were not disastrous. "His voice is pleasant but not one which is rich in nuances," said the *New York Times*. But a scene in which he repeatedly protests "I love you" to his co-star made female moviegoers giggle and critics began to lampoon him. Greta was terrified that her own debut in sound would go the same way, but audiences loved her husky exotic voice from the start. John made one last attempt to get Greta to marry him when she returned from a trip to Sweden in March 1929, but yet again she turned him down. John decided enough was enough. He stopped pursuing Greta and almost immediately became engaged to another actress, Ina Claire. "I hope Mr. Gilbert will be very happy,"

Greta told the reporter who broke the news to her. John and Ina married but, true to pattern, separated within two years. He tried a fourth marriage in 1932 with Virginia Bruce, but they divorced in 1934.

By now, John's alcohol consumption was ruining his health—he had a drinker's red, bulbous nose and glazed eyes, and he frequently vomited blood. Greta still cared deeply about him and tried to help by getting him hired to play opposite her in *Queen Christina* (1933). It was a hit for her and also finally disproved the rumors that John's voice was unsuitable for talkies. But it couldn't save him from himself. He took up with German actress Marlene Dietrich, who hoped to get him a part in a movie with her, but it was too late. In January 1936, at the age of thirty-eight, he had a heart attack and died. Greta was at the theater watching a play when she heard the news and, with typical calm, she stayed till the end of the performance before going home and taking to her bed for several days.

BELOW
By the time the poster was printed, "Garbo and Gilbert" were no longer "in love." "She is capable of doing a lot of damage," John said. "Upsetting thrones, breaking up friendships, wrecking names—that sort of thing."

Greta famously gave up acting in 1941 after *Two-Faced Woman* received bad reviews, and no one was ever able to tempt her back in front of the cameras. Her love life remained mysterious, with several women claiming to have had relationships with her, as well as a few men. Occasionally she was quoted as having made an enigmatic statement, such as "I should prefer to be dead than to love, and I would rather be dead than not to love." She socialized mainly with a crowd of Swedish friends who protected her privacy; anyone who didn't was instantly ostracized. Some of Greta's biographers claim that John was the great love of her life and their affair was the closest she ever came to marrying. Perhaps that is true. But any chance of it working out was destroyed by his overriding love affair with the bottle.

CLARK GABLE

&

CAROLE LOMBARD

WILLIAM CLARK GABLE	JANE ALICE PETERS
BORN: FEBRUARY 1, 1901 CADIZ, OHIO	BORN: OCTOBER 6, 1908 FORT WAYNE, INDIANA
DIED: NOVEMBER 16, 1960 WEST HOLLYWOOD, CALIFORNIA	DIED: JANUARY 16, 1942 POTOSI MOUNTAIN, NEVADA

★

MARRIED: MARCH 29, 1939
KINGMAN, ARIZONA

OPPOSITE
Clark and Carole following their low-key wedding in 1939. She told gossip columnist Louella Parsons, "I'll let Pa be the star and I'll stay home, darn the socks, and look after the kids."

ABOVE
No Man of Her Own
(1932), made while
Carole was struggling
to save her marriage to
Powell. She and Clark
did not get along on
the set.

Would witty, sassy practical joker Carole Lombard manage to
tame America's heartthrob, the womanizing Clark Gable? That was the
question on the lips of everyone who saw them dancing together at
The White Mayfair Ball in January 1936...

Clark Gable was said to have slept with nearly all his costars,
both the famous and the less well-known ones. Joan
Crawford described him as "all man," and their steamy
relationship was known as "the affair that nearly burned Hollywood
down" because of the scandal it caused. Loretta Young got pregnant
with his child in 1935 and sneaked off to England to have the baby, later
pretending to adopt it. The gossip columns were full of his affairs with
starlets, extras, and showgirls and, according to his second wife, he
was like a child who had been given too much candy. However, Carole
Lombard was competitive and wanted nothing but the best, both in
her career and in her marriage. When she set her sights on Clark, who
was nicknamed "The King," she knew she had to challenge him and
not make it too easy or she risked being simply another notch on
his bedpost.

Interestingly enough, they hadn't taken to each other when they
first met on the set of *No Man of Her Own* in 1932. Both were married
to other people and both marriages were in trouble, but he resented
the preferential treatment she got during filming (it was her studio and
he was on loan) so they argued a lot. At the end of the shoot, she gave
him a gift of a ham with his face printed on it and he gave her some
oversized ballet slippers, indicating that he considered her a prima
donna. It wasn't an auspicious start. But when they met again four
years later at The White Mayfair Ball, it
seems they looked at one other with fresh
eyes. And after he danced with her, in her
white silk gown with nothing underneath, she
told friends with a wink that she could tell he
was attracted to her.

*She told friends ... she could
tell he was attracted to her*

Clark invited her to his suite at the
Beverly Wilshire Hotel that evening, but she turned him down with the
line "Who do you think you are? Clark Gable?" The following day she
sent him a peace offering of two white doves in a cage, but whenever
he called to ask her on a date she was busy. The next time they saw

each other she turned up at a party by ambulance and was carried in on a stretcher—a practical joke that Clark told her was in horrible bad taste. It seemed the relationship was doomed before it even started, but then he invited her outside to play tennis in full evening wear, they bantered back and forth across the net as they volleyed a tennis ball, and the ice started to melt. Although she still held him at arm's length, over the next few months they slowly got to know each other—and to fall in love.

SUGAR MAMAS

Clark had a taste for strong women from an early age. His mother died when he was a baby and he was raised by his stepmother, Jennie Dunlap, to whom he was very close. She taught him to play musical instruments and how to speak and dress well, so he stood out from his peers. Clark's father was an itinerant oil driller and then a farmer in Ohio, who tried to instill in his son the value of hard physical work, but at the age of sixteen Clark left home to work in a tire company and soon began to hang around doing odd jobs at the local theater. His father considered acting a career for sissies and they had a huge fight, after which Clark ran away. He auditioned for a theater troupe and attracted the attention of Frances Doerfler, an actress who took him under her wing. She was his first love and helped teach him how to act, but he broke up with her when he met drama-school teacher Josephine Dillon, who was thirty-six to his twenty-two years old. She became his first wife and helped him on the road to stardom by paying for his crooked teeth to be fixed, styling his hair, showing him how to move on stage, and coaching him to lower his high-pitched voice.

Gradually Clark began to get decent parts, and it helped that he was not averse to sleeping with some of the older actresses on the circuit to advance his career. He claimed it wasn't his fault he had affairs because the women chased after him, and that certainly appears to have been the case with Ria Langham, a wealthy forty-three-year-old divorcee. She wanted him as soon as she saw him and used her money to lure him away from Josephine. In 1930, he married Ria, who helped him land leading roles by investing in productions, and who organized Hollywood screen tests for him. "His ears are too big and he looks like an ape," said Darryl F. Zanuck, then head of production at Warner Brothers, but Irving Thalberg offered him a contract at MGM, where his first role was in a movie called *The Easiest Way* (1931). His second appearance was as a bootlegger in *Dance, Fools, Dance* (1931) opposite

Joan Crawford, and heralding the start of their affair. He was usually cast as the unshaven villain or the wisecracking he-man, and the screwball comedy *It Happened One Night* (1934), in which he played an unprincipled reporter, firmly established him as a bankable star. But by this time, the shackles of his marriage were beginning to chafe. Ria ran the household and decided with whom they socialized, while chastising him for his well-publicized flings. In 1935, he moved into a suite at the Beverly Wilshire, although the couple did not divorce. A few months later he danced with Carole Lombard and his head was turned by this lively, sexy woman who swore and played practical jokes just like one of the boys.

Carole was a tomboy, who had grown up with two older brothers and a single mom after her parents separated when she was seven. She liked baseball, football, and boxing, and when she was twelve, she was spotted by director Allan Dawn while sparring with her brothers outside their house and cast in a movie called *A Perfect Crime* (1921). This gave her a taste for acting, and at sixteen she screen tested at Fox and was given a contract. Such a young beauty could have been preyed upon by older lotharios on movie sets, but Carole kept herself out of trouble with her colorful vocabulary and general feistiness. Her route

LEFT
Clark said of Carole, "You can trust that little screwball with your life or your hopes or your weaknesses, and she wouldn't even know how to think about letting you down."

MACK SENNETT'S BATHING BEAUTIES

Canadian-born Mack Sennett set up Keystone Studios in 1912 and became best known for his string of slapstick comedies, involving manic car chases, bumbling cops, wacky accidents, and custard pies in the face. In 1915, seeking to promote his movies, he assembled a bevy of beautiful girls to appear in swimwear alongside his stars, either in films or at promotional events. The showing of bare legs was scandalous in 1915 and he calculated it would guarantee him press coverage. Sennett knew his campaign was working when he started getting hundreds of letters from temperance campaigners complaining that the women were being exploited, and at the same time his box office earnings shot up. The Bathing Beauties proved very popular, becoming pin-ups for soldiers in World War I, then taking part in revues during the 1920s. Many an actress launched her career via this route: Gloria Swanson was a one-time Bathing Beauty, as was Carole Lombard.

to stardom seemed assured until one night in 1926 when she was involved in a car accident in which she was thrown against the windshield of her boyfriend's Bugatti, leaving her with a bone-deep cut from her left cheek to the corner of her mouth. She had plastic surgery to minimize the scarring and she studied makeup and lighting effects to help disguise it, so that by the time she returned to the screen, the injury was barely noticeable.

During 1927-28, Carole made thirteen slapstick comedies with Mack Sennett, in which she developed her comic timing as well as using her athleticism. She had a lovely silvery voice and moved seamlessly into talkies, signing a five-year contract with Paramount in 1930, around the same time Clark was signing with MGM. During the filming of *Man of the World* (1931) she fell for the leading man, William Powell, who was sixteen years older than she was, and they married, coincidentally just a week after Clark married Ria Langham. Their happiness was short-lived, however. Carole cabled friends the morning after their wedding night, saying "Nothing new to report." Powell was a serious man, who objected to her liberal use of profanities, and the marriage was doomed from the start. Carole's next boyfriend, Russ

RIGHT
Carole with her by-then ex-husband William Powell in My Man Godfrey *(1936). She said they were "two completely incompatible people."*

Columbo, died after a tragic shooting accident in 1934, and she threw herself into her career. She knew she loved playing comedy and organized a string of wacky parties to persuade the studio honchos to cast her in comic roles. It worked, and she became Hollywood's queen of screwball comedy, in films such as *Hands Across the Table* (1935) and *Love Before Breakfast* (1936). But once she started dating Clark Gable, her career was no longer the most important thing in her life. For once, she decided to put a man first.

THE HAPPY COUPLE

"He had my number so fast it was terrifying," Carole told a friend about Clark. He saw through the extroverted comedienne exterior and found she was a deeply loyal, generous person underneath. Everyone liked her, from the doormen to the studio bosses. "She's more fun than anybody, but she'll take a poke at you if you have it coming and make you like it," Clark said. They both enjoyed horse-riding and spent their Sundays at rodeos and horse shows, playing tennis, or at boxing or wrestling matches. In the evenings, they attended parties and premieres, and soon gossip was buzzing about the new pairing. Carole made Clark take it slowly, because apart from anything else they both had "morals" clauses in their contracts and he was still married. He always said he knew he was in love with her when he watched her performance in *My Man Godfrey* (1936), in which she played a zany socialite who hires a tramp to become her butler, then falls in love with him. Clark asked Ria for a divorce, but she demanded so much money that he refused to pay. That meant he couldn't be seen to cohabit with Carole, or Ria would be able to divorce him on the grounds of his infidelity. They were stuck in an impasse.

Carole moved to a secluded house in Bel-Air, which they called The Farm, so Clark could visit her discreetly and with any luck elude the private detectives his wife had hired to tail him. He taught Carole

"He had my number so fast it was terrifying"

ABOVE
Clark Gable in Gone with the Wind. *Conscious of his public image he tried to get out of doing the scene in which Rhett Butler cries after hearing of Scarlett's miscarriage, but the director insisted and Carole thought the result was the best acting he ever did.*

how to fish and shoot ducks, and for three years they conducted their affair without being caught *in flagrante* by Ria's detectives. They were both at the top of their game in Hollywood. He was reluctant to take on the role of Rhett Butler in *Gone with the Wind* (1939), but it would make him a household name for generations to come. She received an Oscar nomination for *My Man Godfrey* and in 1937 became Hollywood's highest-paid actress when she agreed to a new deal with Paramount. Their personalities were quite different, with him the more quiet and easygoing while she was the boisterous joker, but she made him the center of her universe. She became his buddy as well as his lover, and began to eschew glitzy parties in exchange for quiet nights at home. The practical jokes continued, though. When it came to a good gag, nothing was too much trouble for Carole. British director Alfred Hitchcock had once said that actors were like cattle in his hands, so

ABOVE
Carole and Clark on their 20-acre ranch in Encino, where they kept horses, cows, chickens, turkeys, and a mule.

when he arrived on set to start filming *Mr. and Mrs. Smith* (1941), he found Carole had installed a pen with three live calves in it bearing the names of each of the movie's stars. And Clark was often on the receiving end of gags, once finding a blow-up woman in his bed when Carole was away from home.

In January 1939, *Photoplay* magazine published an article entitled "Hollywood's Unmarried Husbands and Wives," naming Clark and Carole as one of the couples, and MGM piled the pressure on Clark to divorce. Finally, he agreed to pay Ria over half a million dollars and the divorce was finalized on March 8, 1939. The next day that Clark was clear of filming commitments was March 29 and the couple "eloped," slipping out of Hollywood and marrying in the small town of Kingman, Arizona. Carole wore a light gray suit created for her by the popular designer Irene, while Clark wore a blue serge suit. There was no time for a honeymoon; they drove back to Hollywood, stopping for their wedding dinner at a roadside restaurant, where diners were delighted to get autographs signed "Carole Gable." She told gossip columnist Louella Parsons that all she wanted now was to be a good wife and give Clark a child. Tragically, that was something she would never be able to do.

ABOVE
"Hollywood's Unmarried Husbands and Wives."
This infamous Photoplay article of January 1939, listed Clark and Carole alongside Robert Taylor and Barbara Stanwyck, Gilbert Roland and Constance Bennett, and George Raft and Virginia Pine. *The first three couples quickly got married after publication, but George couldn't marry Virginia because he was already married to a Catholic woman.*

THE WAR BONDS TRIP

Right after Japan bombed the American fleet at Pearl Harbor and America entered World War II, Clark and Carole wrote to President Roosevelt offering to help the war effort in any way they could. They became key figures in the Hollywood Victory Committee and Clark headed the division that selected actors and actresses to take part in rallies and tours of troop encampments and hospitals. One of the first requests in early 1942 was to send a movie star to Indiana to help promote the state's US Defense Bonds (loans to the government to fund the war), and Clark decided that Carole should go since Indiana was her home state. It was a decision he would come to regret for the rest of his life.

Carole was a huge success with the crowds in Indianapolis, holding up her arms in a V for Victory sign, and giving her autographed picture to everyone who bought bonds. Her quota was $500,000 but she raised $2,017,513 with her patriotic performance. She was there for a week and immediately afterward, she wanted to rush straight home

RIGHT
Carole attracted huge crowds to buy defense bonds: on the morning of January 15, 1942, 3,000 people stood in line in State House, Indianapolis, with no idea that less that twenty-four hours later Carole would be dead.

to Clark. It's rumored they had quarrelled just before she left because she suspected he might be having an affair with his costar Lana Turner. Perhaps she was keen to make up and that's why she insisted that the party, including her mother and Clark's best man, Otto Winkler, should fly back on the overnight flight instead of catching the train, which would take three days. The flight touched down to refuel several times and as it took off from its last stop, Las Vegas, it flew directly into the peak of the 8,500-foot-high Mount Potosi and all on board were killed instantly.

Clark got news of the crash at eight the following morning, around the time he was expecting Carole home. He dashed to the foot of the mountain and watched as their remains were brought down on stretchers. A pair of diamond and ruby earrings he had given Carole for Christmas were recovered from the site. He was in a state of shock and disbelief and it took him some time to accept that she had gone. He went back to finish the movie with Lana Turner, but, she reported "I've never known anyone to suffer so much." He lost 20 pounds and his blood pressure became so high the doctors warned him he had to stop drinking spirits.

Carole was posthumously awarded a medal as "the first woman to be killed in action," and Clark decided to honor her memory by signing up for the war. He trained as an officer and undertook some flying missions in Europe, where Hitler, who was a huge fan, offered a reward to anyone who could capture him alive. But being in action couldn't mend Clark's broken heart. He returned to work in Hollywood and married twice more, trying with each wife to find a replica of Carole. When he died of a heart attack in November 1960, he was buried next to her at Forest Lawn cemetery in the Hollywood Hills.

HOLLYWOOD FOR VICTORY

Three days after Pearl Harbor, the Hollywood Victory Committee was formed to rally the movie industry in support of the war effort. Clark Gable was nominated to head the Screen Actors Division, and he accepted immediately. The first meeting was held on December 22, 1941, and Carole Lombard attended wearing a black silk dress and telling everyone she'd come disguised as a blackout. There were several strands to Hollywood's campaigns: the studios produced patriotic films for at-home audiences; many stars made personal appearances at bond rallies or volunteered for the Red Cross; and some, most famously Bob Hope, toured overseas military camps to raise troops' morale. In 1942, Bette Davis was one of the founder members of the Hollywood Canteen, in which servicemen and women could enjoy free refreshments served by the stars, and could even enjoy a dance with one of the celebrity volunteers. In its first year, it attracted more than a million guests.

LEFT
Carole was posthumously awarded a Medal of Freedom.

SPENCER TRACY

&

KATHARINE HEPBURN

SPENCER BONAVENTURE TRACY

BORN: APRIL 5, 1900
MILWAUKEE, WISCONSIN

DIED: JUNE 10, 1967
BEVERLY HILLS, CALIFORNIA

KATHARINE HOUGHTON HEPBURN

BORN: MAY 12, 1907
HARTFORD, CONNECTICUT

DIED: JUNE 29, 2003
FENWICK, CONNECTICUT

RIGHT
There would never be any cozy domestic photos of Spencer and Katharine except for movie stills. This still is from Woman of the Year *(1942), their first movie together.*

ABOVE
"His ears stuck out. And he had old lion's eyes. And he had a wonderful head of hair. And a sort of ruddy skin, really like mine," was Katharine's affectionate description of Spencer's appearance.

RIGHT
Katharine's father invested her earnings and made her a very rich woman, but still she would "make do and mend," and search for little economies around the house.

OPPOSITE
Spencer on the cover of a magazine in 1940, the year before he met Katharine, when he was drinking heavily. He referred to his period of alcoholism as "the ol' heimerdeimer days."

They were Hollywood's unlikeliest couple: Katharine the eccentric New England schoolmarm type who exercised daily, took cold showers, and always knew best about everything; Spencer the on-again/off-again alcoholic and depressive with an Irish Catholic background—and a wife he refused to divorce.

O n paper, Spencer and Katharine had very little in common, but they both had strong, influential fathers who thought acting was not a suitable career choice, despite their showing an aptitude for it in their early years. Spencer was addicted to the movies as a boy, but when he left school he briefly considered becoming a priest before joining the Navy during World War I, only for hostilities to cease before he had qualified for active service. Next he went to Ripon College, Wisconsin, planning to study medicine, a path approved of by his Irish father, John, who ran a company that sold trucks. However, at Ripon Spencer got involved first with the debating society and then started to act—and before long he had been bitten by the acting bug. His father thought he'd gone soft, but he won a scholarship to the American Academy of Dramatic Arts in New York City and all thoughts of medicine left his head.

After he graduated in March 1923, Spencer struggled to get theater work and was on the verge of giving up the profession when influential director George Cohan gave him a role in a play called *Yellow*, and told him, "Tracy, you're the best goddamned actor I've ever seen." His fortunes changed after *Yellow* was a huge hit and in 1930, when agents from Fox movie studios came knocking, Spencer was happy to make the move to Hollywood. It took a few years and a few box-office flops, but in 1936 he had a hit with *Fury*, directed by Fritz Lang, then *San Francisco*, for which he received an Oscar nomination, and in 1937 he won his first Oscar for his role in *Captains Courageous*.

Spencer was an actor's actor. Contemporaries marveled that he didn't use tricks or props but was simply able to inhabit a role. "The thing about his acting is there's no bullshit in it,"

"Tracy, you're the best goddamned actor I've ever seen"

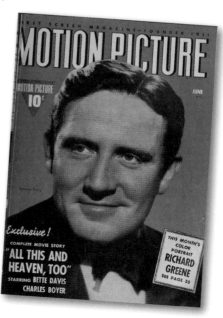

explained his friend Humphrey Bogart. When asked the secret of his talent, Spencer replied, "I learn the lines." But all was not rosy in Spencer's private life. Soon after graduating from college he had married fellow actor Louise Treadwell, whom he met while they were both working in a stock company called White Plains, and in June 1924 their son, John, was born. When John was ten months old, Louise accidentally let a porch door slam next to the baby's cot and was surprised that he didn't respond to the noise. She took him for tests and learned that the boy was profoundly deaf. The news was so distressing that she couldn't bring herself to tell Spencer for three months while she researched the condition for herself. At the time he was having an affair with another actress and was devastated when he was told the news, feeling that the boy's disability was somehow his fault, a kind of punishment for his transgressions. The shock made him turn increasingly to alcohol and throughout the late 1920s and the decade that followed he was frequently drunk on stage and on movie sets. He also had a long string of affairs with leading ladies, including

BELOW
Spencer with Joan Crawford in Mannequin (1937). "At first I felt honored to be working with Spence," she said, "and we even whooped it up a little off the set, but he turned out to be a real bastard." In other words, he didn't fall in love with her.

Loretta Young, Joan Crawford, and Ingrid
Bergman. He moved out of the marital
home but continued to visit and support
his family financially. Louise gave up her
own career to devote herself to John and
their daughter, Susie. She taught John
how to lip-read and then how to speak,
researching all the latest treatments for
the deaf in the hope that her son would
one day lead a normal life. Spencer and
Louise announced their separation to
journalists in 1933 but insisted they
would stay friends. There was no
question of a divorce, and if anyone so
much as mentioned the "d" word Louise
insisted, "I will be Mrs. Spencer Tracy
until the day I die." Spencer's Catholic
guilt about his infidelities, his drinking,
and his son's deafness meant that he
would do whatever she wanted.

ABOVE
*Katharine and Spencer
in* Keeper of the Flame
*(1942), in which he
played a journalist who
comes to interview a
young widow after the
death of her husband.*

A FORCE OF NATURE

In 1941 Spencer agreed to make a movie called *Woman of the Year*,
produced by Joe Mankiewicz and costarring Katharine Hepburn.
When he arrived on set, Joe introduced them and, according to legend,
Katharine's first words to him, uttered with a friendly smile, were, "Mr.
Tracy, I believe I am too tall for you." (He was 5'10½" to her 5'9".) The
director quipped, "Don't worry, honey. He'll soon cut you down to size."
She said later that she found Spencer irresistible rightaway but was
worried that she wasn't attractive enough for him. His affair with the
incandescent Ingrid Bergman had been widely reported, and Katharine
knew she couldn't compete on looks, but from that first day they
started having lunch together in the studio parking lot and found they
got along like a house on fire. Spencer's first impression was that she
might be a lesbian, perhaps because she wore pants in an era when it
was still not socially acceptable for women to do so, but he soon found
out she was just a uniquely independent freethinking woman.

Katharine's father was a leading urologist and a campaigner for
better sexual health, while her mother agitated for women to have the
vote and easy access to birth control. When Katharine was two, the

STREET & SMITH'S

PICTURE PLAY

MAY 1933

KATHARINE
HEPBURN

THE STRANGE CASE
OF
BOB MONTGOMERY

ABOVE
A magazine cover in
May 1933, by which time
Katharine was based in
Hollywood. She wouldn't
buy a property there
but only rented, always
considering the East
Coast her true home.

leading British suffragette Emmeline Pankhurst came to stay in the family's Connecticut home, and when she was four her mother took her along when she picketed the White House and made soapbox speeches about women's enslavement to domesticity. Katharine had an older brother, Tom, and four younger siblings, and free expression reined in the household, with meals often becoming impromptu debating chambers. They were an active family and the children all learned to climb trees, swim in raging seas, cycle up hills, ride horses, and play a range of sports. Katharine reportedly shaved her head, annoyed that boys sometimes pulled her hair and determined to deny them the opportunity. She dressed in her brother Tom's cast-off clothes and considered herself as tough as any boy. But when she was thirteen a deep shadow fell across the happy childhood. She and Tom had been spending Easter at a friend's house in Boston, and on the Sunday morning she found Tom hanged in the attic. He was only fifteen, with no motive to commit suicide, and Katharine always believed that he was trying to emulate a scene in a play they'd seen the week before, in which a man was hanged from a tree. It changed her, for one thing making her lose any belief in life after death, and for another making her fiercely private.

After school, Katharine went to Bryn Mawr College, Pennsylvania, as her mother had done before her, and achieved acclaim for her acting in college productions. Her father tried to dissuade her from pursuing an acting career, but she was determined, even when many of her early shows received hostile criticism. Dorothy Parker famously said of her performance in The Lake (1933), "Katharine Hepburn runs the gamut of emotions from A to B." But Katharine was not someone who gave up easily. Hollywood director George Cukor saw a screen test and gave her a role in the film A Bill of Divorcement (1932). She arrived on the West Coast to sign a long-term contract with RKO, leaving behind her husband of four years, Ludlow Ogden Smith, a businessman she had met while still a student. An affair with her agent, Leland Hayward, followed, but he was married so it didn't go anywhere. For two years from 1936–38 she was involved with millionaire Howard Hughes, who reportedly wanted to marry her, but by that stage Katharine had turned against the whole idea of marriage and children. "I would have been a terrible mother," she said, "because I'm basically a very selfish human being."

Her movie career floundered after a few duds, and the trade press began to label her "box office poison," but far from giving up Katharine went back to the stage. Howard bought her the rights to a new play called *The Philadelphia Story*, and this became first a massive hit show, stretching to 417 performances in its first run, and then an equally successful movie. The role of the socialite Tracy Lord, whose wedding plans are disrupted by the arrival of an attractive journalist, completely revived Hepburn's career, but still when she met Spencer in 1941, there was no question that he was the more famous of the

HOWARD HUGHES

Heir to a multimillion-dollar fortune that his father had created through the Hughes Tool Company, Howard used his inheritance to launch a career as a Hollywood producer. His very first movie, *Two Arabian Nights*, won the Academy Award for 1927, and his next, *Hell's Angels*, led to his developing an interest in aviation and starting his own airline company. On September 13, 1935, he set a world speed record by taking the H-1 plane up to 352 miles per hour, and three years later he piloted a plane all the way around the world. He was notoriously promiscuous and had affairs with dozens of Hollywood stars of the era, including Ava Gardner, Bette Davis, Olivia de Havilland, and Ginger Rogers. Katharine lived with him during their relationship but moved out after discovering he was being unfaithful. "Love for him had turned to water," she wrote in her autobiography. Howard continued to make movies and was the owner of RKO studios for a time in the 1940s, but he suffered from a form of obsessive-compulsive disorder that became increasingly severe as he got older, and lived his final years as an eccentric recluse.

LEFT
Hughes's round-the-world flight took just three days, nineteen hours—knocking four hours off the previous record.

two. Reviewers noted they had terrific on-screen chemistry in *Woman of the Year*, in which they played a feuding couple. They would make nine movies together over the next twenty-six years, with Katharine often playing the high-class, stuck-up girl who was brought down to earth by the diamond-in-the-rough character of her leading man. She always claimed her association with Spencer helped tremendously to advance her career—but of even greater importance was his role in her personal life.

Although Spencer was not drinking at the point when they met, he was overweight from an addiction to candy and he seldom took any exercise. Ever the doctor's daughter, Katharine felt the urge to take him in hand: "I wanted him to be happy—safe—comfortable. I like to wait on him—listen to him—feed him . . ." she wrote in her autobiography. She fussed around him like a mother hen, and he ribbed

BELOW
"You see, the trouble with Kath is that she understands me," Spencer told friends.

her about her fancy New England ways: "Christ, you talk like you've got a feather up your ass all the time!" he teased. He obviously liked her quirkiness and the way she took care of him, but he also made it clear to her that he would never divorce Louise; out of respect for her they agreed not to appear together in public except when making or promoting their movies, and never to give interviews about their private life. They couldn't dine out in restaurants or arrive together for premieres. They socialized discreetly but kept separate homes. And the press largely respected their privacy, although gossip columnists couldn't stop themselves from dropping heavy hints about the "secret love" in Miss Hepburn's life—a story that would often be juxtaposed with an item about Spencer Tracy. Katharine had soon fallen passionately in love with Spencer. "It was a unique feeling . . ." she said later in life. "I would have done anything for him."

CARE & NURTURE

Katharine and Spencer lived a simple life. When he was filming, she would pick him up from the studio, drive him to her place, prepare dinner, then take him home again. Sometimes she would invite friends over, so long as they weren't heavy drinkers, but despite her precautions it wasn't long before Tracy's demons reared up and he started binge drinking again. According to friends, he was a nasty drunk, and Katharine later admitted that he hit her at least once, but she was quick to make excuses for him. "I'm like a little fly that buzzes around him all the time, and every once in a while he gives me a good swat." She considered his problems with alcohol a failure of willpower and tried to get him to drink moderately, just a couple of glasses a night, but for someone with raging alcoholism this proved impossible. When she realized her plan wasn't working, she encouraged him to swap his rowdy excesses for safer pursuits, such as watercolor painting, walking on beaches, and flying kites. Whenever he went on a binge, she'd move him into her house until he had sobered up again. She could be bossy and bloody-minded, so there were frequent fireworks. "He was so steady and I was so volatile that we exasperated each other. And we challenged each other, and that was the fun of it." But they fitted together. The arrangement worked.

ABOVE
Pat and Mike (1952) in which she played a champion sportswoman and he was a sports promoter. The script was written by friends of theirs, Garson Kanin and Ruth Gordon, to capitalize on Katharine's athletic abilities.

Spencer still visited his family regularly, and in 1942 when Louise decided to open a school for deaf children, he agreed to back it financially. For the first year, he was the sole sponsor and thereafter wrote checks of $20,000 to $30,000 a year to support the award-winning John Tracy Clinic. Katharine stayed in the background and was often absent for long periods when filming—in Uganda and the Congo in 1951 making *The African Queen*, and in London in 1959 making *Suddenly, Last Summer*—and she also continued to do theatrical tours in New York, Australia, and England. During her absences, Spencer was not always entirely faithful, but on her return they'd always be reunited again.

KATHARINE HEPBURN'S RULES OF HEALTHY LIVING

"Dad believed health to be the most important factor in success, and exercise the most important in health," Katharine explained. Into her eighties she played tennis daily (and she played ferociously), swam constantly, rode her bike in Central Park, walked, jogged, and ran. Until the demands of her career got in the way, she had been one of America's top women golfers. She believed firmly in the importance of sleep and was known to sleep up to fourteen hours a day. She took seven or eight freezing-cold showers a day and had peculiar notions about diet, including the belief that you should always eat a cooked fruit with every meat dish, and that you should lie on the floor after meals to aid digestion. She loved giving medical advice to friends with ailments, and woe to them if they did not follow her instructions to the letter. When friends asked Spencer over dinner one evening how he kept his own health so good, he replied, with a wicked glance across at Katharine, "Well, I take three awful hot baths every single day and I eat *nothin'* but fried foods!"

RIGHT
Katharine played both golf and tennis to near-professional standards and was fiercely competitive.

And then on July 31, 1963, they were together having a picnic on a Los Angeles beach when Spencer collapsed with severe breathing difficulties. Katharine got him to the hospital, where he was diagnosed with chest congestion caused by chronic heart problems. When he was discharged, she moved into his Beverly Hills house where, for the next four years, she would look after him, putting her career on hold. They had a separate phone line installed, so there was no risk of Katharine answering the phone when his wife called. She nursed him and reminded him to take his medication. By 1967 he seemed well enough to return to the screen and appeared with Katharine in *Guess Who's Coming to Dinner*. Just days after filming finished, on the night of June 10, Katharine heard Spencer getting up and going to the kitchen in the middle of the night. As she walked through to see what he wanted she heard the sound of a cup smashing on the floor. When she pushed open the door, she found Spencer collapsed at the table, already dead from a massive heart attack. He was sixty-seven years old.

Out of respect for Spencer's wife, Katharine decided not to attend his funeral. Instead, she went to the undertaker's that morning, watched as they lifted his coffin into the hearse, then followed it in her own car for six miles, only turning off as the procession approached the church. A few days after the funeral, she telephoned

Louise and introduced herself, saying, "I hope we can be friends," and offering to help the family if she could. "I thought you were only a rumor," Louise replied sharply. The dig must have hurt Katharine. She moved back to Connecticut to live with her assistant, Phyllis Wilbourn, and continued working right into her eighties.

According to British director Anthony Harvey, "When she lost Spence, the center of her life was destroyed." She could never bear to watch *Guess Who's Coming to Dinner*. She didn't speak openly about Spencer until after Louise died in November 1983, but then began to give a few interviews and eventually wrote her autobiography, *Me: Stories of my Life*. "Spence was the only pure person I ever met," she wrote. "He had no affectations—not a selfish bone in his body . . . I'll miss him every day as long as I live." She admitted that he had never told her he loved her in so many words, but said she guessed he must have to put up with her for twenty-six years.

> *"He had no affectations— not a selfish bone in his body . . . I'll miss him every day as long as I live"*

BELOW
On the set of Guess Who's Coming to Dinner (1967). When asked why she stayed with Spencer so long, Katharine replied, "I honestly don't know. I can only say that I could never have left him."

LAURENCE OLIVIER

&

VIVIEN LEIGH

LAURENCE KERR OLIVIER

BORN: MAY 22, 1907
DORKING, ENGLAND

DIED: JULY 11, 1989
WEST SUSSEX, ENGLAND

VIVIAN MARY HARTLEY

BORN: NOVEMBER 5, 1913
DARJEELING, INDIA

DIED: JULY 8, 1967
LONDON, ENGLAND

★

MARRIED: AUGUST 31, 1940
SANTA BARBARA, CALIFORNIA

OPPOSITE
Laurence kisses Vivien after hearing she has won an Academy Award for her performance in A Streetcar Named Desire, *March 1952. Greer Garson accepted the Oscar on her behalf as Vivien was appearing on stage in New York at the time.*

ABOVE
*Vivien was a
breathtaking beauty but
was insecure about her
large hands and tried
to disguise them by
thrusting them in her
pockets, wearing gloves,
or folding her arms.*

Laurence was perfectly happy in his marriage to Jill Esmond until Vivien set her sights on him. Even before their first meeting she told friends she would be the next Mrs. Olivier and, faced with the determination of such an indescribably beautiful young woman, he failed to resist.

*L*aurence's father was a stern High Anglican priest who ruled the household with a rod of steel, and the young boy was terrified of him. He was close to his mother, but she died when he was thirteen and he later wrote of the bereavement, "I was nearly destroyed." His mother had often encouraged him to act, to overcome his physical awkwardness —"As a child I was a shrimp, as a youth I was a weed"—and he appeared in school plays as well as being a choirboy at his father's church in Dorking, Surrey. After his mother's death he was sent to boarding school in Oxford, but was confused about which career to choose, considering the navy or farming as options until his father told him categorically that he should be an actor. He attended the Central School of Speech and Drama in London, then found work with the Birmingham Repertory Company, taking on minor roles at first and gradually landing bigger parts as his talent was recognized. In 1928 he appeared in a production of *Bird in the Hand* by John Drinkwater, with a slender, pretty actress named Jill Esmond. Her initial indifference spurred him to pursue her and when the show transferred to New York without him, he sought work there just to be near her. He had to propose several times but finally she agreed to marry him in July 1930.

Over the next few years, Jill put her career on the back burner to follow Laurence as he made his name in the English theatrical world and dipped a toe into

BELOW
Laurence at the age of twenty-three, in the year he married Jill. He had matinee-idol looks and had just signed a movie contract with producer Alexander Korda.

> *She smiled a devastating smile, looking directly at him with her kittenish blue-gray-green eyes*

movies, although it was still a medium he held in low regard. He had grown into a handsome man and many costars pursued him but he remained faithful to Jill, his stability, his rock. They were good friends who read scripts together and discussed the best ways to approach parts, and the icing on the cake came in 1935, when Jill announced she was pregnant. Neither had any inkling that the predatory young Vivien Leigh had developed a serious crush on him after seeing him in a string of performances that year and was even then plotting how to seduce him.

Vivien heard that the Oliviers liked to eat in London's Savoy Grill, so she began to frequent the restaurant whenever she could. One evening in December 1935 she was there with a friend when she spotted the couple and went over to introduce herself. She grasped Laurence's hand tightly and smiled a devastating smile, looking directly at him with her kittenish blue-gray-green eyes. He smiled back, slightly baffled, and wished her well with her career, before continuing with his meal.

THE HUSBAND-STEALER

Vivien was born in Darjeeling, India and lived there until the age of six with her Roman Catholic mother and her cavalry officer father. She was upset at being sent to board in a convent just outside London, missing the color and exoticism of India, but she soon made friends and told everyone she would be a great actress when she grew up. The convent was strict—a white chemise had to be worn while bathing to cover one's own naked body, and patent shoes were banned in case men might see up a girl's skirt from the reflection, but Vivien was an obedient child who did not rebel. Her parents agreed to send her to the Royal Academy of Dramatic Art (RADA) but soon after starting there she met a lawyer named Herbert Leigh Holman at the South Devon Hunt Ball and fell in love. He was thirteen years older than she was, a serious man who didn't want his wife to act, but nevertheless in December 1932 she married him.

Vivien left RADA and had a child, Suzanne, in 1933, but still retained her acting ambitions. Against her husband's wishes, she found a manager, John Gliddon, and together they came up with the stage name Vivien Leigh (a combination of her own and her husband's

names). She spent hours in front of the mirror practicing facial
expressions, particularly conveying emotion with the eyes and
eyebrows, which she had been told was the key to success in the
movies, but it was in a play, *The Mask of Virtue* (1935), that she first
received critical recognition. She got the role because beauty was the
main requisite, but the reviews were so universally glowing that the
newspapers called her the "fame-in-one-night girl." Director Alexander
Korda, having previously turned her down, admitted he had made a
mistake and gave her a five-year contract to appear in his movies.

When Vivien met Laurence in the Savoy, he had heard of her and
was generous in his praise. Soon afterward, she went backstage to
congratulate him after watching his masterful *Romeo and Juliet*, in
which he alternated the roles of Romeo and Mercutio with John
Gielgud, and he invited her to lunch. Much to her disappointment he
brought Gielgud along, but as a result of that lunch, she auditioned and
got a role in his *Richard II*. It wasn't until summer 1936, when she played
his lover in the movie *Fire over England*, that she and Laurence spent
time together between takes and he began to fall for her, while his wife
Jill was pregnant. After filming finished and his son was born, he took
Jill for a vacation in Capri, but Vivien hurried out to Italy to bump into
them as if by accident. The two women couldn't have been more

BELOW
*Laurence and Vivien
in 1937. Actress Phyllis
Konstam, who knew
them both, said, "No
one could have been
more wicked than
Vivien. She set out quite
deliberately to destroy
that marriage [between
Laurence and Jill]."*

different: Jill was calm and easygoing, while Vivien was witty and
mercurial. Seeing them together, Laurence realized he had fallen
in love with Vivien.

Everyone warned Vivien not to steal Laurence from his wife and
baby son: her mother, his friends, her friends. Jill was friendly to her
and could never bring herself to beg her not to take her husband,
and when Larry and Vivien were in Denmark together in 1937, acting
in a production of *Hamlet* at Elsinore, they both made the decision to
leave their marriages. Herbert hadn't known about the affair so it came
as a shock, and both he and Jill refused the divorce petitions at first.
It wasn't until 1940 that the legal paperwork finally went through,
citing Laurence and Vivien as co-respondents and giving custody of
their children to their former spouses. At one minute past midnight on
August 31, 1940, the very first minute it was legally possible, they wed
at San Ysidro Ranch, Santa Barbara.

TEACHER & PUPIL

Vivien didn't just love Larry; she worshipped him. To her, he was the
greatest actor alive, and she hung on his every word when he taught
her about acting. Together they watched people they encountered
in everyday life and analyzed their tiniest gestures. He taught her to
anticipate what an audience wants and then refuse to give it to them,

so they wouldn't get too comfortable. "If you do it right you feel it," he told her. "It takes something out of you and puts something in, as all emotional experiences do." She was more widely read than he, more knowledgeable about art and music, but when it came to acting he was the master and she his adoring pupil.

He went to Hollywood in 1938 to take the role of Heathcliff in *Wuthering Heights*; disappointed that Vivien had not been cast as Cathy, he clashed with costar Merle Oberon during filming. Vivien flew out to visit him for five days but they couldn't be openly together since the divorces hadn't gone through. It was during this trip that she won the role of Scarlett O'Hara in the epic *Gone with the Wind*. When it was released, she got glowing reviews—the *New York Times* said "Vivien Leigh's Scarlett is so beautiful she hardly need be talented, and so talented she need not have been so beautiful"—and she won the Best Actress Oscar in 1939, while Olivier was nominated but didn't win for his Heathcliff (he won his first Oscar for his performance in *Hamlet* in 1948).

THE SEARCH FOR SCARLETT

In her bestselling novel *Gone With the Wind*, Margaret Mitchell described her heroine as having "green eyes in the carefully sweet face turbulent, lusty for life, distinctly at variance with her decorous manner." When David O. Selznick began looking for his Scarlett for the screen version, it was this duality he had in mind but he failed to find it in a search that took two and a half years and cost $100,000. He saw 1,400 hopefuls, including all the big names of the day, among them Bette Davis, Joan Crawford, Tallulah Bankhead, and Katharine Hepburn. Jean Arthur, Joan Bennett, and Paulette Goddard were the front-runners when Selznick was forced by his bosses to start filming without having cast his leading lady. But Olivier's American agent happened to be the director's brother, and he took Vivien along to the set just as they finished filming the burning of Atlanta. "Here is your Scarlett," he announced. Vivien looked up with her enchanting, slightly mischievous smile and the part was won.

Olivier in the title role in Richard III (1955). He is said to have based his characterization on a theater director named Jed Harris who was universally despised. Years later, he was amused to find out that Disney animators had also used Harris as a model when creating the character of the Big Bad Wolf.

Even if Laurence felt slightly piqued at her win, they were still wildly in love, and friends described their "sexual greediness" for each other. They stayed in America, where they socialized with the great and the good of Broadway and Hollywood. Their star was firmly in the ascendant, despite a production of *Romeo and Juliet* in New York that they both funded and appeared in, but which turned out to be an almighty flop. When World War II began, Olivier signed up for the Royal Air Force and took flying lessons, but he was never called upon to serve and they spent most of the war years working in theater and film in the UK. In spring 1944, Vivien was overjoyed to discover she was pregnant, but in midsummer she became violently ill while filming G.B. Shaw's *Caesar and Cleopatra*, and lost the baby. This provoked a terrifying bout of mental illness, in which she first of all became acutely depressed and anxious before turning on Laurence one night, attacking him both verbally and physically. After about an hour, she collapsed in hysterical sobbing on the floor and wouldn't let him come near. The next day she had no recollection of what had happened and was profusely apologetic when he described her behavior, but she refused to see a doctor. It was alarming, but Larry hoped against hope that it was a one-time occurrence.

Later in 1944, Vivien consulted a doctor about a persistent cough that had been troubling her and was found to have tuberculosis in one lung. For several months, she had to rest at their home, the 17th-century Notley Abbey, and threw herself into renovating the house and grounds, but during this period there were more attacks of her mysterious mental illness. Vivien was terrified she was going crazy and frantically worried about letting Laurence down. He figured out that attacks were precipitated by a period of intense activity, and

sometimes excessive alcohol consumption, but had no idea how
to cope with them. His life centered around his work and he hated
emotional scenes of any kind, so he decided the best course of action
was for both of them to keep busy.

His career was blooming, with dazzling successes in his movie
version of *Henry V* and his stage roles in *Richard III* and *The School for
Scandal*. He became a director of London's Old Vic theater, and in 1947
was awarded a knighthood, after which the couple would be known as
Lord and Lady Olivier. He and Vivien undertook a six-month tour of
Australia and New Zealand later that year, which left her utterly
exhausted, but on her return she got the part of Blanche DuBois in
Tennessee Williams's *A Streetcar Named Desire*—first on the London
stage, then in New York, and finally in the 1951 movie. Her performance
as the faded beauty with a promiscuous past was highly acclaimed and
won her another Oscar, but it also left her mentally fragile and the
attacks became more frequent.

BELOW
*Vivien Leigh and Marlon
Brando in* A Streetcar
Named Desire *(1951).
She was convinced she
had to become a great
actress in order to earn
Laurence's love.*

Then in 1953, while filming *Elephant Walk* in Ceylon, Vivien tipped
over the edge into a full breakdown. She
had an affair with her co-star Peter Finch
and began following him around the
set, sobbing hysterically and reciting
Blanche DuBois's lines. On the flight
home, she took her clothes off and tried
to jump out of the aircraft. Once back
in the UK, she was admitted to hospital
where a variety of treatments were
tried—electric shocks, ice packs
applied to the body, being fed on
raw eggs—that now seem bizarre or
even grotesque but were all standard
procedures for the day. Laurence was
distraught. He could no longer reach
her and he felt the great love they had
shared was slipping away. He clung to
the hope that she could be cured, but
his feelings for her were changing
from love to deep pity. She was still
the exquisite creature he had adored,
but how could their marriage ever be
the same again?

METHODS OF ACTING

Olivier didn't enjoy making movies at first and his theatrical style often seemed overstated on screen. During the filming of *Wuthering Heights* (1939) director William Wyler coached him on how to make his acting more subtle. When approaching any new part, Olivier's technique was to use a costume, a way of walking, or a mannerism as a key to the character, and he worked instinctively, without overanalyzing. He was scornful of actors who studied "the Method," based on the teachings of Constantin Stanislavski and popularized by Lee Strasberg at his Actors Studio in New York. Method actors analyze the character's background and psychology and draw on personal memories to immerse themselves in the role, to the extent that some almost live through the experiences and can find it hard to let go after filming stops. When he made *The Prince and the Showgirl* (1957) with Marilyn Monroe, Olivier criticized her Method acting. When he made *Marathon Man* (1976) with Dustin Hoffmann, and the latter didn't sleep for three nights since that was what his character had been through, Olivier said "Try acting, dear boy. It's much easier."

RIGHT
Laurence playing washed-up music-hall star Archie Rice.

MADNESS & MAYHEM

Vivien came back to recuperate at Notley Abbey, but from then on Laurence never knew when she might turn on him again. If things were good, she was a fabulous hostess, throwing glamorous parties and impressing guests with her wide general knowledge. There was gossip that she was having affairs but Laurence simply shrugged them off and detached himself emotionally for the sake of self-preservation. Vivien desperately wanted to give him a child, convinced that would heal their marital problems, but a miscarriage in 1956 brought on yet another cycle of her mental illness, which was now diagnosed as manic depression.

In 1957, Laurence took on the role of music-hall performer Archie Rice in *The Entertainer*, which became one of his most famous parts, and his daughter was played by a young unknown called Joan Plowright. Vivien was utterly astonished when she heard rumors that he and Joan were having an

affair, simply because she considered Joan to be so plain. At the same time she realized that Joan was young enough to give him children, and she wasn't. She still loved him desperately but couldn't stop the terrible attacks that were damaging their relationship so irreparably.

In 1958, Vivien began an affair with an actor named Jack Merivale, with whom she was appearing in New York in a play called *Duel of Angels*. All the same she was deeply distressed when Laurence wrote asking her for a divorce. She got several friends to beg him not to leave her and indicated she would accept any terms he wished to impose in order to save their marriage. But it was too late. Laurence told Joan that his life with Vivien had been one of "violence, passion and shattering longing," but with her he felt only "gentle tenderness and serenity." The divorce went through in 1960, after twenty years of tempestuous marriage, and then, in 1961, Vivien became distraught at the news that Laurence and Joan had married. She believed everything was Joan's fault and would never hear a word said against her ex-husband, telling a friend that she "would rather have lived a short life with Larry than a long life without him."

ABOVE
Laurence and third wife Joan. Their marriage lasted twenty-eight years, until his death in 1989, but was not always smooth sailing. She said, "If a man is touched by genius, he is not an ordinary person. He doesn't lead an ordinary life."

Jack Merivale proved a loyal companion and he was living with Vivien in May 1967 when her tuberculosis recurred. She seemed to recover but on the night of July 7, Jack found her collapsed on the bedroom floor. She'd got out of bed and her lungs had filled with fluid, causing her to drown.

"This—this was love," he sobbed. "This was the real thing"

When he heard the news, Laurence rushed over immediately and stood by her lifeless body "praying for forgiveness for all the evils that had sprung up between us." They had been theatrical royalty, the golden couple whom it seemed nothing or no one could ever part. Laurence continued to work and had three children with Joan but in 1982, a friend found him, now in his seventies, watching one of Vivien's movies on television and weeping. "This—this was love," he sobbed. "This was the real thing."

FEDERICO FELLINI

&

GIULIETTA MASINA

FEDERICO FELLINI

BORN: JANUARY 20, 1920
RIMINI, ITALY

DIED: OCTOBER 31, 1993
ROME, ITALY

GIULIA ANNA MASINA

BORN: FEBRUARY 22, 1921
SAN GIORGIO DI PIANO, ITALY

DIED: MARCH 23, 1994
ROME, ITALY

★

MARRIED: OCTOBER 30, 1943
ROME, ITALY

RIGHT
Federico and Giulietta in Venice. She was his touchstone, the bedrock of his life. Inset: poster for Luci del Varietà (Variety Lights, 1950), starring Giulietta.

"It is only when I am doing my work that I feel truly alive," said Federico. He was a great visionary whose movies would influence many other directors.

In wartime Rome, Federico and Giulietta fell deeply in love and decided they wanted to spend the rest of their lives together. But three tragedies, one after the other, changed the nature of their relationship into one that was less conventional and even more profound.

*U*nlike virtually all other Italian boys, the young Federico had no interest in soccer, and despite the fact that he grew up in the coastal town of Rimini, he never learned to swim. Instead, this rather solitary child liked playing with puppets and painting portraits. At the age of seventeen, he and a friend set up what they called the Funny Face Shop, where they drew caricatures or cut out silhouettes of customers from black paper. He was a talented cartoonist who bombarded the satirical magazine *420* until they published some examples of his work. His parents wanted him to study law and with that purpose in mind he enrolled at a college in Rome, but it appears he didn't take it terribly seriously as there is only evidence of him taking a few of the exams. He should have begun his national service in 1939, but resorting to a series of ingenious ruses (fake health problems, dual residences, and so forth) he managed to get out of it. Then, in the summer of 1942, he began cowriting skits for EIAR (the Italian radio corporation) with a friend. His first one started with a man asking another man for a light for his cigarette, and ended with the first man walking off with the other's cigarette, jacket, pants, and girlfriend. This was fun—much more fun than law.

By this time, Federico had already survived his first heartbreak. In 1936, he fell for Bianca Soriani, a girl who lived opposite his family home in Rimini. Both sets of parents were against the match and in 1938 Bianca's family moved to Milan and the couple split up, but there's no doubt it was a grand passion for Federico. He once passed out during an argument with his parents about Bianca, such was the strength of his feelings. Shortly after her departure, a friend took him

BELOW
Giulietta in La Strada *(1952), one of her most memorable roles. Federico once said, "For me, a clownesque talent in an actor is the most precious gift she can have."*

to a brothel where he had his first sexual experience, an encounter that left him with an "anxiety about sex," according to the friend. He was certainly no Casanova back in those days, but when in the fall of 1942 he was introduced to Giulietta in the corridors of EIAR, he was immediately attracted to her and had sufficient confidence to telephone her. He asked if she could supply a photograph so that he could consider her for a role in a movie he was planning—and then he asked her to lunch.

A BRIEF COURTSHIP

Giulietta's father was a classical violinist and her mother a teacher in the small town of San Giorgio de Piano, near Bologna. From her early school years, she grew up in Rome, keeping her aunt Giulia company after the death of her uncle. Aunt Giulia was an inspiring figure who took her niece to the theater and encouraged her to take singing and dancing lessons. Young Giulietta was a happy, extroverted girl who studied literature and archeology at the university in Rome and got involved in student theater productions before deciding she wanted to be an actress. In 1942, she joined the Compagnia del Teatro Comico Musicale and played various roles for them before she bumped into the tall, dark-haired, rather handsome Federico at EIAR. She was eager to get into radio because there was more money to be made there than in theater.

When Federico invited her to lunch she accepted, thinking it might be fun to try her hand at movie acting. She couldn't let her aunt know, as going out with a boy unchaperoned would have been considered scandalous, so she ate one lunch at home with her aunt then another with Federico. He took her to a high-class restaurant in Rome's Piazza Poli, and she worried he might have made a mistake and wouldn't have the funds to pay, but when the bill arrived he pulled out a large wad of cash and settled it. Giulietta would later joke that it was the last time in their lives she ever saw him with so much money, as he was notoriously profligate.

The relationship was serious from the start. There was no game-playing. They simply chose each other and knew they wanted to be together. She later described him to a journalist as a "dear genius" with "deep eyes, restless, inquisitive." He gave her the nickname Lo Spippolo (meaning a small thing that inspires tenderness) because she was such a tiny, elfin creature. Federico was a huge believer in chance and always said that their meeting was predetermined and could not have turned out differently. They complemented each other perfectly. She was driven while he was a dreamer. She believed in mapping out a path and following it, while he was more of a drifter. She made him laugh and he felt protective because she was so good-natured and trusting. But when it came to work, both were perfectionists who understood each other's visions, and it was this that would create such a strong partnership through the years ahead.

GREAT JOY & DEEP SORROW

Giulietta and Federico married in 1943 after a nine-month courtship, on the very day that the papers announced all men between the ages of seventeen and thirty-seven were being called up to fight in the war. Federico was twenty-three and still dodging the draft. For this reason, their wedding ceremony was held in Aunt Giulia's apartment rather than in a church, which would have drawn attention to them. A prelate who lived in the same building conducted the ceremony, using a corner cabinet as an altar. Neither set of parents could attend because of the fighting that raged throughout the Italian peninsula, and there were only a few guests. Federico drew an elaborate series of drawings for the invitation, with cartoon versions of both of them kneeling in the middle of a heart alongside intersecting paths—and an empty road sign containing a space for the name of the baby she was already expecting. After the ceremony, they went out to watch an afternoon show at the Galleria theater before beginning their married life hiding out in the attic of Aunt Giulia's house so he could avoid military service.

Everything was wonderful. They had each found their soulmate and chatted excitedly about the future—all the movies they were going to make together, as well as the children they would have. Once the war was over, nothing would stand in their way. But then, disaster

BELOW
Giulietta's first impressions of Federico: "He looks like a fakir, reminds me of Gandhi." His of her: "She's a little rascal, I like her very much, she makes me laugh."

struck. A few months after the wedding, Giulietta fell downstairs and lost the baby she'd been carrying. They were distraught. Within a few months she was pregnant again and the baby, a boy they named Pierfederico, was born on March 22, 1945. However, their much-wanted child was born with encephalitis, an inflammation of the brain, and lived for just one month and two days. Meanwhile, after the birth Giulietta came down with puerperal fever, a severe infection of the reproductive organs that meant she would never be able to conceive again. The couple mourned together and according to friends they became spiritually closer but their physical relationship ended around this time. This may have stemmed from her strong religious faith, which preached that the only purpose of sex was procreation, or perhaps she had a fear of intercourse after everything she had been through. Whatever the reasons, their relationship changed fundamentally.

A LOVER OF WOMEN

Federico's movie career began when he was asked to write gags for other people's scripts, most notably for *Rome, Open City* (1945) and *Paisà* (1946), directed by Roberto Rossellini. He had immense energy and a passion for cinema, and quickly proceeded to writing and directing his own films in the Italian neorealist style, starting with *Variety Lights* (1950), which starred Giulietta. It wasn't particularly well-received but a couple of years later *La Strada* (1952) established Federico as a name to be reckoned with, winning more than fifty international awards including the Oscar for Best Foreign Language Film. It featured Giulietta in one of the most memorable roles of her career as Gelsomina, a naive young girl who goes on the road with a cruel traveling strongman. She was hailed by critics as a "female Charlie Chaplin" for her performance, which combines both innocence and pathos. She even wears a bowler hat, just like the Little Tramp himself. During filming, Federico fell into a deep depression and started seeing a Jungian analyst, a process he found absorbing and one that would feed into later autobiographical movies, such as *8½* (1963) and

Amarcord (1973), particularly with his use of dream sequences. The triumphs kept coming; he would win the Oscar for Best Foreign Language Film five times altogether, and he frequently won the Palme d'Or at Cannes, the Silver Lion at Venice, and the Golden Globe in the US. He was an actor's director and coaxed career-best performances from his favorites, particularly Marcello Mastroianni (with whom he made six movies) and Giulietta (with whom he made five). No one could have been more delighted than he when Giulietta won the Cannes prize for Best Actress in 1957 for her role in *Nights of Cabiria*, in which she plays a prostitute searching for love.

The couple worked so closely together that there were inevitably conflicts at times, but Federico relied

CINECITTÀ

In 1937, Benito Mussolini founded Rome's world-famous film studios, which would become closely associated with Federico as the place where he shot some of his most famous movies, including *La Dolce Vita*, *Satyricon*, and *Casanova*. The studios were bombed during the war and became a refugee camp for some years afterward, but the facilities survived and since the 1950s have hosted many international productions as well as home-grown ones. *Quo Vadis* was filmed there in 1951, and the producers of *Ben Hur* (1959), starring Charlton Heston, were able to reuse some of the earlier Roman sets. Elizabeth Taylor and Richard Burton fell in love there while making *Cleopatra* in 1962; Franco Zeffirelli made *Romeo and Juliet* there in 1968; and Martin Scorsese recreated the streets of New York within Cinecittà's walls for *Gangs of New York* as recently as 2002. Over the years it has faced bankruptcy and threats of closure, fires, and floods, but its Fascist-styled architecture still stands.

on Giulietta's instinctive judgments. "When he was working on an idea, I never asked him anything because he was very protective about his work in the creative phase," she once said in an interview. "Afterward, however, he always came to look for me to show me his ideas, his scripts, his drawings, and asked me what I thought." She was his muse, his partner, the woman who ran his home and managed his life for him. But she was not his lover in the physical sense and Federico was a man who loved women, so from early in their marriage he had affairs.

There was Lea Giacomini from San Marino, who was driven to despair by him and ended up in a mental hospital. There was a pharmacist called Anna Giovannini, who met Federico in a bakery in 1957 and became his mistress for the rest of his life, giving up her work so as to be available to him whenever he chose to call on her. There was Sandra Milo who played the sexy mistress in 8½ (a role based on Anna Giovannini) and claimed that she and Federico had "seventeen years of love" together. In 1975 he had a brief affair with feminist author Germaine Greer. And he may have had a fling with actress Eleonora Duodati in the final year of his life. Federico loved pretty, voluptuous women (the opposite type from the petite tomboyish Giulietta) and got a reputation for pouncing on them, given half a chance. Anita Ekburg, immortalized when she danced in the Trevi Fountain in *La Dolce Vita*, claims he leaped on her in a hotel room and she only escaped by pretending to have acute appendicitis.

RIGHT
Federico with Sandra Milo, the sexy mistress in 8¹/2, who was one of his lovers. He called her Bamboccia, which means "happy doll."

What did Giulietta make of all this? She didn't know about all the women he bedded, but she certainly knew about some and went to incredible efforts to keep stories out of the press. She knew how to work with Rome's paparazzi (so-called after a character Federico had invented in *La Dolce Vita*) and was largely successful in preventing them from writing about her husband's affairs. When photographs appeared in November 1971 showing Federico with Anna Giovannini, the text inferred that she was an actress appearing in one of his movies rather than spilling the beans about their long-term affair. Some of his movies seemed to mirror real life, though, such as *Giulietta degli Spiriti* (1965), which featured his wife playing a middle-aged woman trying to decide whether to leave her philandering husband, and in which he cast Sandra Milo as a mistress. All the same, Giulietta was incensed when Sandra Milo published an autobiography discussing her affair with Federico, and the marriage appeared to be on shaky ground for a while. Other mistresses were discreet enough to keep their counsel, or at least not to talk about their affairs till long after Federico and Giulietta were dead. Anna Giovannini only revealed the secret of her thirty-six-year affair with him in 1995, and Germaine Greer waited until 2010 before telling of her own brief encounter. Giulietta may have been the long-suffering wife, but she always knew Federico would never leave her for any of these women. As a family friend who was also a priest later explained, "Giulietta wasn't only his support; she was his breath."

"*Giulietta wasn't only his support; she was his breath*"

A LIFETIME OF ACHIEVEMENT

During the 1960s, Giulietta added another string to her bow when she became the host of a popular television show called *Lettere aperte* (Open Letters) in which she answered questions sent from viewers on such matters as what to do about a husband who abandoned his family, or a son who refused to marry the girl his parents chose. The letters and her responses were published in a best-selling book in 1975. But the crowning glory of her husband's career came in 1993 when Federico was awarded an Oscar for Lifetime Achievement. He had been suffering from ill health, and they weren't sure if he would be able

ABOVE
Drawing was Federico's first love, and he always sketched the characters in his movies as a way of fixing their qualities in his mind.

MARCELLO MASTROIANNI

All great directors have their favorite actors and for Federico, besides his wife, it was Marcello Mastroianni, the handsome, charismatic man whom perhaps he saw as a kind of alter ego. They first worked together on *La Dolce Vita*, with Federico having to fight his backers to cast this relative unknown over the studio's choice of Paul Newman. They collaborated on five more movies, with Mastroianni usually playing a tortured, complex character who was often a womanizer. They visited each other's families, made fun of each other, and were secretly jealous when the other worked with other people. In Federico's autobiographical masterpiece *8¹/₂* Mastroianni played the film director himself. Like Federico, the actor had a complex private life, reportedly having affairs with a number of famous women, including Faye Dunaway, Catherine Deneuve, Lauren Hutton, Ursula Andress, and Claudia Cardinale. However, unlike Federico, his affairs were usually plastered all over the international press.

RIGHT
Marcello Mastroianni with Sophia Loren: they made many movies together, but she was one of the few co-stars he was never able to bed.

to make the journey in person to pick up his award, but he decided to risk it. On March 29, 1993, he walked onto the stage at the Dorothy Chandler Pavilion to accept the award from his compatriots Sophia Loren and Marcello Mastroianni. Explaining that he didn't have time to thank all the people he would like to thank in the time available, he mentioned just one—his wife. "Thank you, dear Giulietta," he said, "and please stop crying." The cameras panned around to show her with tears of joy streaming down her cheeks.

Soon after the Oscar ceremony, Federico's health began to fail. He had heart-bypass surgery in June and suffered a stroke in August. Meanwhile Giulietta was diagnosed with lung cancer, and the two suddenly found themselves installed in separate hospitals. On October 17, Federico was allowed to leave the hospital to have lunch with Giulietta and some friends. She was wearing a turban to conceal the baldness caused by her chemotherapy, and he was very frail, but it was a happy occasion all the

same. Afterward they visited an office Federico was hoping to move into upon his release, and he asked his friends to bring him some paints, brushes, and an easel so he could return to his first love, painting. Then he was taken back to the hospital and that night fell into a coma from which he would never awaken. He died the day after their fiftieth wedding anniversary. Giulietta attended his funeral looking very frail, and blew kisses and waved at his casket as it was carried out of the church. Just five months later she followed him to the grave.

Theirs was an unconventional marriage but possibly all the stronger because of its focus on the spiritual and intellectual rather than the physical. "Not having children has made us the sons and daughters of each other, as fate would have it," she said. In fact, they were much more than that; children leave one day and make their own lives, but Federico and Giulietta were partners till the very end. "Our first meeting? I do not remember it," Federico said late in life, "because in fact I was born the day when I saw Giulietta for the first time."

> *"I was born the day when I saw Giulietta for the first time"*

ABOVE
*"When you live with another person for 50 years, all of your memories are invested in that person, like a bank account of shared memories . . . It is better than any scrapbook because you are both living scrapbooks."
So said Federico of his marriage to Giulietta.*

HUMPHREY BOGART

&

LAUREN BACALL

HUMPHREY DEFOREST BOGART

BORN: DECEMBER 25, 1899
NEW YORK CITY

DIED: JANUARY 14, 1957
HOLLYWOOD, CALIFORNIA

BETTY JOAN PERSKE

BORN: SEPTEMBER 16, 1924
NEW YORK CITY

★

MARRIED: MAY 21, 1945
LUCAS, OHIO

OPPOSITE
Betty and Bogie on their wedding day. "A lot of broads in this town, but I married a lady with class," he said proudly.

ABOVE
According to actress
friend Dorris Bowden,
"Everyone adored Betty.
She was pretty, she was
quick-witted, and sharp."

RIGHT
Warner Brothers
originally saw Bogie
as "a tough guy, not a
ladies' man," but the
fans who mobbed him at
any public appearances
certainly thought he
had sex appeal.

Bogie was forty-four and looked older after years of hard living. Betty was nineteen and looked younger when she was plucked straight from a modeling career to be groomed for stardom. No one could have guessed they would fall for each other, but one day while they were joking around in her dressing room he cupped his hand under her chin and kissed her.

H umphrey Bogart was often cast as the rough-edged villain from the wrong part of town, but in fact his parents were well-off and he had a privileged upbringing in New York City's Upper West Side, where his father was a doctor and his mother an advertising illustrator. A picture his mother drew of him as a baby was used in Mellins Baby Food adverts, but otherwise she didn't pay much attention to her children, while his father became addicted to morphine, making him distant and unaffectionate. Later in life, Humphrey said, "A kiss in our family was an event." He was sent to prestigious schools and his parents hoped he would go on to Yale and become a doctor, so they were disappointed when he flunked out and volunteered for the army in 1918, whereupon he was assigned to convoy duty across the Atlantic. Upon returning, his route into theater came via a family friend, and he tried his hand at writing and directing before deciding his talents lay in acting. His breakthrough role was in Robert E. Sherwood's *The Petrified Forest* (1936) and when Warner Brothers bought the movie rights he was whisked out to Hollywood to appear as Duke Mantee, the gunman. Reviews hailed his performance as the "subnormal, bewildered, and sentimental killer," and he was put under contract with Warners.

By this time, Bogie (as he became known) was on his second marriage and heading for his third. Perhaps it was the lack of love in his childhood that made him a serial husband. He didn't sleep his way around the studio, as many other stars did, but tended to marry all the girls he had long-term relationships with. The first was Helen Menken, a Broadway costar who married him in 1926 then divorced him a year and a half later on grounds of cruelty, claiming he hit her. His next union—with another actress, Mary Phillips—went well at first, but when he moved to Hollywood and she continued to work in New York, the periods of separation damaged the marriage. It wasn't long before he met buxom blonde Mayo Methot while filming *Marked Woman* (1937), and the following year she became wife number three. Bogie told a

journalist he was marrying her because "I love a good fight. So does Mayo," and they soon became known as "the Battling Bogarts" due to their drink-fueled feuds. He nicknamed her "Sluggy" and their home "Sluggy Hollow," but in fact her alcohol consumption was no joke. She could drink Bogie under the table, and her violence became ever more extreme. On one occasion she stabbed him, and she frequently threw glasses at his head (although he claimed he didn't bother to duck, because her aim was so bad). Bogie persuaded Mayo to go to a doctor, who diagnosed her as an alcoholic with paranoid schizophrenic tendencies. To Bogie's credit, rather than leave he felt a sense of responsibility to stay and try to help her.

The decline of this third marriage coincided with the ascent of his reputation as an actor and box-office star. *High Sierra* (1941) marked his last major gangster role and thereafter he moved into more complex, interesting parts, such as the private eye Sam Spade in *The Maltese Falcon* (1941) and Rick Blaine in *Casablanca* (1942), his first romantic lead. During the filiming of *Casablanca* he had to stand on a box or sit on cushions because Ingrid Bergman was taller than he was, but it showed he could play a romantic lead convincingly.

In 1943, director Howard Hawks introduced him to Betty, a young unknown to whom they had given the stage name Lauren Bacall, telling him that they would like her to star opposite him in *To Have and Have Not*. Under the terms of his contract, he had approval of his leading ladies, and he looked at the shy, nervous, undeniably gorgeous Betty and gave his consent, commenting later, "She's a very long girl" (she was 5'8", the same height as he was, and very slim). If he was attracted to her, he didn't let on. There was a twenty-five-year age difference between them, and his home situation was far too complex. An affair would only make matters worse.

THE FLIRTATION PERIOD

Betty was the only child of a Jewish-Romanian mother and a Polish father who left home when she was five. Her mother wasn't well-off, but an uncle paid for Betty to attend a good school, where a friend remembers her as "a determined young lady with a will of iron." It was this gritty determination that would get Betty the lead in a Hollywood movie when she was still in her teens and had no professional acting experience. First she worked as a model for department store advertisements, while taking acting classes on Saturday mornings and supplementing her income by working as a theater usher and selling a showbiz newspaper. "She was a knockout in those days," an ex-boyfriend remembered, "with a laugh, delivery, and a great sense of humor." She was sighted by Diana Vreeland, a columnist at *Harper's Bazaar* magazine, and a small picture of her appeared in the January 1943 issue, where it was noticed by the wife of Howard Hawks. At that time the director was looking for a girl to cast in *To Have and Have Not* and, thinking that she looked like a young Marlene Dietrich, he offered Betty a ticket to Hollywood to do a screen test. To try and control her nerves, Betty tilted her head down and looked up at him with her doe eyes, a characteristic of hers that later became known as "The Look." Although her acting in

> " *A determined young lady with a will of iron* "

front of the camera left a lot to be desired, Hawks decided to mentor her. First he got her to lower her voice, then coached her in acting techniques, before personally directing her screen test. He undoubtedly had a crush on her, but it was destined never to be consummated.

On March 6, 1944, filming began on *To Have and Have Not*, and Betty later recalled that "there was no clap of thunder" between her and Bogie. Instead they became friends who joked around with each other, such as the time he handcuffed her in her dressing room while the rest of the crew went out for lunch. Gradually, almost imperceptibly, they were spending more time together and then the moment came when he first kissed her. Howard Hawks was jealous when they were seen holding hands on the lot and warned Betty that she meant nothing to Bogart, leading to an angry confrontation between the two men. Word of the flirtation got back to the volatile Mayo, who began phoning the set constantly, asking Bogie, "How're you doing with your daughter? She's half your age, you know." There's no doubt that Bogie was something of a father figure to Betty, giving her advice on acting and the ways of Hollywood, but she also loved the fact that he was so well-read, and such fun to be with. "I was older than nineteen in many ways," she said, "and he had such energy and vitality he seemed to be no particular age." He and Betty sneaked off after filming to eat hamburgers in his car or walk on the beach, but still he went home to Mayo. Betty was content to be his mistress and made no demands of him while he struggled with his conscience. Bogie left Mayo twice in 1944, driven out by arguments, but he still felt an obligation to help her and returned when she promised to stop drinking. Finally, at Christmas that year, enough was enough and he left for the final time. At last he was free to be with Betty openly, and it came as a huge relief.

Betty was in New York at the end of January 1945 when she was confronted by reporters who told her that Bogie had said they were engaged. "That's the first I've heard of it," she commented, in her now deep, husky voice. But when he did propose, her answer was a foregone conclusion, and on May 21 they were married in a friend's farmhouse in Lucas, Ohio. As they sipped their drinks after the wedding, Bogie told the judge who'd presided over the ceremony, "I feel more married today than I did the three other times." He was with a different kind of woman now, one who would become the wife he had always wanted.

A SUPPORTING ROLE

When they first married, Bogie was Betty's god, but she was no pushover and it wasn't long before she was stamping her own personality on the marriage. She persuaded him to move to a big house in Benedict Canyon, which had previously belonged to Hedy Lamarr, where they entertained frequently and with great generosity. Director John Huston said of her, "She was adorable to Bogie and his friends, and she was always warm, charming, and dear." She didn't particularly enjoy outings on his beloved boat, the *Santana*, as she suffered from seasickness, but in all other respects she fitted in with his lifestyle and did what she could to make him happy. They appeared together in thrillers *The Big Sleep* (1946) and *Dark Passage* (1947), then in *Key Largo* (1948), with her usually playing a ballsy dame who doesn't give a damn. She turned down scripts she didn't like, despite being under contract because, for her, being Bogie's wife was her most important role. Their son Stephen was born in 1949 and a daughter, Leslie, in 1952. "I always wanted a career," she later told a biographer, "but I also always wanted a home of my own, a husband, and children.

BELOW
Betty and Bogie in the classic film noir The Big Sleep *(1946). The plot is so complicated that the producer wired Raymond Chandler, author of the novel on which it is based, to ask who killed the chauffeur—and even he didn't know!*

THE AFRICAN QUEEN

The story of an English missionary (played by Katharine Hepburn) who persuades a hard-bitten riverboat captain (Bogie) to take her out of German territory at the beginning of World War I was shot mainly in remote parts of Congo and Uganda, and it was a challenging shoot to say the least. The extreme humidity meant costumes were quickly covered in green mildew, the rivers on which they sailed were crocodile-infested, their camp was attacked by a plague of giant soldier ants, the boat they were using for filming sprang a leak and sank, and another one caught fire and began to drift downriver toward a steamer ship full of passengers, whereupon Bogie managed to rescue them. The food was so atrocious that at one stage Betty took over and arranged for edible meals to be flown in. And everyone got dysentery apart from Bogie and director John Huston, who attributed their good health to the fact that they drank Scotch rather than water.

I made up my mind long ago that when I did find them, they would come first."

Betty was completely behind her husband when he flew to Washington, D.C., in October 1947 to support the so-called Hollywood Ten, a group of screenwriters who were blacklisted for their alleged support of communism. His gesture backfired when he was accused of communism himself

and had to write an article distancing himself from the Ten or risk losing his Hollywood career in those days of growing anticommunist hysteria. In 1952, Betty campaigned for democrat Adlai Stevenson in the presidential election and defined herself as a "staunch liberal"—"You are welcoming to everyone when you are a liberal. You do not have a small mind." Her strength of character was evident to all during the filming of *The African Queen* in the Congo in 1951, when she cooked and washed clothes for the cast and crew and nursed people who fell ill. Bogie's role as a hard-boiled riverboat captain would win him a Best Actor Oscar.

The key to the success of their marriage is that, unlike his third wife, Betty didn't fight him. There were tensions at times, often caused by his drinking, and Betty later said, "You had to stay awake married to him . . . He liked keeping people off balance . . . I could never be quite sure what he would do." She was no pushover, but if she wanted something she learned the best ways to persuade him of it. Both of them had a great sense of honor and wouldn't tolerate lies, even when the truth wasn't necessarily what the other person wanted to hear. And when rumors reached Betty that her husband was having an affair with Verita Peterson, his hairdresser, during filming of *The Barefoot Contessa* in Rome in 1954, she didn't smash plates or threaten divorce: instead she is said to have gone on a very expensive shopping spree to all her favorite designer stores.

SHEER ANIMAL COURAGE

Betty's most important supporting role began in January 1956 when Bogie was diagnosed with throat cancer. She slept on a cot in his hospital room after he had surgery to remove the growth, then nursed

THE RAT PACK

Just after Christmas 1955, the Bogarts met some friends for a celebration at Romanoff's restaurant in Beverly Hills. Betty looked around at the degenerate, intoxicated bunch and said, "I see the rat pack is all here." The name stuck and they decided to make formal appointments to the crew. Frank Sinatra became pack master, Judy Garland was first vice president, Betty was den mother, Sid Luft (Garland's husband) was cage master, and Bogey was "rat in charge of public relations." David Niven, Spencer Tracy, Katharine Hepburn, Cary Grant, and Rex Harrison were also listed among the members. According to an official notice they placed in the *New York Herald Tribune*, the pack had no specific purpose apart from "the relief of boredom and the perpetuation of independence." The Rat Pack continued after Bogie's death, with new members in the 1960s including Dean Martin and Sammy Davis, Jr. They had a reputation for heavy drinking and chasing women, but as one member said, "Do you believe these guys had to chase broads? They had to chase 'em away."

RIGHT
Betty dances with fellow Rat Frank Sinatra, but is quoted as saying of him, "I wish Frank Sinatra would just shut up and sing."

him at home as he battled the illness with what director John Huston described as "sheer animal courage." As the treatments progressed and he became sicker and the pain got worse, she hid her own grief and continued to be bright and cheerful, inviting friends over to visit every afternoon. When he could no longer walk, he got downstairs by wheeling his wheelchair into a dumbwaiter in their home. Newspaper reports that he was close to death infuriated him and he frequently called the editors to berate them. Among regular visitors were David Niven, Frank Sinatra, Richard Burton, Truman Capote, and director George Cukor. On Saturday, January 12, 1957, his close friends Katharine Hepburn and Spencer Tracy stopped by, and when Bogie clutched his pal Spencer's hand and said "Goodbye" instead of "Goodnight," they both knew what it meant. Betty slept on his bed that night and in the morning of the 13th she slipped into a coma. The following day, the 14th, he passed away. Betty told a friend, "The bottom dropped out of my life." He had been her anchor, her best friend, her great love, and now she was adrift without him.

In her despair, Betty had an affair with Frank Sinatra, one of Bogie's Rat Pack buddies, but the relationship ended after she told a friend he had proposed and the story reached the gossip columns. In 1961 she married actor Jason Robards and they had a son, Sam. But they divorced in 1969, a breakup she attributes in her autobiography to his alcoholism. In both cases it appears she was trying to find a substitute for Bogey, the man who had been the core of her life, but no one could step into his shoes and she didn't marry again.

In the second half of her life, she achieved notable successes in her acting career, winning a Tony Award for *Applause* on Broadway in 1970 and later being nominated for an Academy Award for her role in *The Mirror Has Two Faces* (1996). Hollywood acknowledged her contribution to film with an Honorary Award in 2009. She also won the National Book Award for her autobiography *By Myself* (1980). She had a good life without Bogie, but always said he had shaped her and made her who she was. "I don't know what would have happened to me if I hadn't met him," she said in 2005. "He changed me, he gave me everything. And he was an extraordinary man."

" *He changed me, he gave me everything. And he was an extraordinary man* "

ROBERTO ROSSELLINI

&

INGRID BERGMAN

ROBERTO GASTONE ZEFFIRO ROSSELLINI

BORN: MAY 8, 1906
ROME, ITALY

DIED: JUNE 3, 1977
ROME, ITALY

INGRID BERGMAN

BORN: AUGUST 29, 1915
STOCKHOLM, SWEDEN

DIED: AUGUST 29, 1982
LONDON, ENGLAND

★

MARRIED: MAY 24, 1950
ROME, ITALY

PICTURE POST

BERGMAN AND HER DIRECTOR
Ingrid Bergman and Roberto Rossellini
on the Italian Island of Stromboli

PRINCE CHARLES:
40 PAGES **HIS FIRST SIX MONTHS** **4**D

OPPOSITE
*Roberto and Ingrid
in 1953, the year they
made Journey to
Italy, a film portrait
of a marriage. Inset: a
paparazzi shot shows
them sailing to the
island of Stromboli
in 1949, at the start
of their affair.*

Ingrid said that although
he died when she was
thirteen, "It was to my
father's enthusiasm for
my pretending and my
acting as a little girl that
I owe everything."

Studio publicists promoted Ingrid as a wholesome Swedish beauty with an idyllic family life, so the American public was scandalized when she left her doctor husband and their twelve-year-old daughter to run off with Roberto, a married Italian movie director with a womanizing reputation—and whose child she was already carrying.

ehind every happy family photograph there is a story that doesn't necessarily match the smiling image. Ingrid Bergman had a tragic childhood, full of loss: her mother died when she was two, her beloved father when she was thirteen. She went to stay with an aunt, who only months later suffered a heart attack and died in her arms while Ingrid was waiting for help to arrive. To compound the tragedy, her uncle had been calling from the street for her to throw him the key to the building, but the girl was unable to hear him through the closed window. Ingrid couldn't shake the guilt of forgetting to open the window that day, and would forever blame herself for her aunt's death. She spent the remainder of her teens living with another aunt and uncle and some cousins, but perhaps it wasn't any wonder that she got married at the age of twenty-two to the first man she ever dated. After all the trauma of her early life, she yearned for security and a stable home.

Petter Lindström was eight years older than she was, a good man,
a dentist just beginning to train as a surgeon. Ingrid was sure she was in love, saying in her autobiography, "I felt very romantically about him," but on their wedding night the sex was disappointing. "Perhaps it was because we had come to know each other too well before we married, becoming almost like a brother and sister." No matter. Ingrid assumed that sex wasn't all it was made out to be and was determined to make herself a

BELOW
Just after Ingrid's eighteenth birthday, a cousin set her up on a blind date with Petter Lindström. She saw him as a man-of-the-world and felt very shy and self-conscious.

good wife and a good mother to their daughter Pia, who was born in
1938. Her parents had been very much in love, so much so that they
waited seven years before marrying while her father toiled away
making enough money to win his in-laws' approval. Ingrid wanted her
own marriage to be a beautiful love story just like theirs.

THE HOLLYWOOD YEARS

Her route to stardom was relatively straightforward. She won a place at
Stockholm's Royal Dramatic Theater School, worked in theater and as
an extra, then began to land movie roles. The Swedish movie industry
in the 1930s was very technically advanced and Hollywood scouts kept
an eye on their output. When Ingrid played a pianist who has an affair
with a famous violinist in *Intermezzo*, (1936), she was spotted by Kay
Brown, an assistant of director David O. Selznick, who invited her to
New York to remake the movie in English. She sailed for America in
April 1939 and remade *Intermezzo* with Leslie Howard playing her lover;
the movie was an overnight success with both critics and public. A new
star was born, with everyone acclaiming Ingrid's naturalness in front of
the camera, her purity, and her superlative beauty. She had resisted
being "made over" by the Hollywood stylists, refusing to let them pluck
out her eyebrows and redraw them in pencil as so many stars did in
those days, so she looked like a real flesh-and-blood woman on screen.

Selznick offered her a seven-year
contract with his own studio, Selznick
International Pictures, and Petter and
Pia came out to join her in Hollywood,
where he was able to practice as a
doctor and advise on her career.

Ingrid didn't really want to make it,
but *Casablanca* (1942) was the movie
that would lodge her firmly in the
memories of fans for decades to come.
She preferred *For Whom the Bell Tolls*
(1943), based on the Hemingway novel.
In 1944 she won her first Oscar for her
role as a wife being driven to madness
in *Gaslight*. Every movie she appeared
in was box-office magic; it seemed she
couldn't put a foot wrong. But behind
the scenes, her "perfect marriage"

HITCHCOCK'S BLONDES

Ingrid Bergman was in good company as one of the cool blonde leading ladies favored by British director Alfred Hitchcock. Among the others were Janet Leigh (she of the famous shower scene in *Psycho*), the ever-glamorous Grace Kelly (*Rear Window*, *To Catch a Thief*) and Tippi Hedren (who fought off giant crows in *The Birds*). Hitchcock explained in an interview that he favored "the drawing-room type, the real ladies who become whores once they're in the bedroom," adding that he liked that element of surprise. He was notorious for treating actors badly, making them do multiple takes of the most difficult, uncomfortable scenes, but Ingrid was a consummate professional and had nothing but good to say about him. She recalled asking him one day about her motivation in *Spellbound* (1945) as an intelligent woman who throws everything away for love. "Fake it, Ingrid," he said. "It's only a movie." And then five years later, as fate would have it, she found herself throwing everything away for love.

was in trouble. Petter had become hypercritical, often scolding her for eating cookies or ice cream and telling her she needed to lose weight. They stopped communicating and the cracks began to widen. It was at this point that she was invited to Paris to entertain US troops based there and met the war photographer Robert Capa. He was an extraordinary man, already famous for his coverage of the Spanish Civil War and his photos of American troops landing on Omaha Beach on D-Day, 1944. They had a passionate love affair and for the first time Ingrid felt her sexuality awakened. He warned her that he would never marry her because he was too committed to his work, but some advice he gave her would soon change the course of her career. As she later recounted, "He cautioned me about falling into the trap of doing what was easy and well paid, and brought glory. He told me if I did so, I wouldn't feel fulfilled."

On her return to Hollywood, Ingrid met director Alfred Hitchcock and their happy collaboration led to three hit movies, but with Capa's words ringing in her ears, she started looking around for something more. One afternoon in 1948 she went to a movie theater and watched *Rome, Open City*, a movie by a director

ROME, OPEN CITY

Rossellini started making a movie about the German occupation of Rome within a month of the tanks rolling out in June 1944. He sold his furniture and borrowed money from a wealthy elderly lady to part fund the movie, which was shot on location in the streets so recently devastated by fighting. His light came from a cable run across the road between a betting shop and a newspaper office, and he secretly plugged his leads into their electricity supplies. When he ran out of film, he persuaded a soldier in the US Army Signal Corps, Rod E. Geiger, to purloin more for him. Most of the actors were nonprofessionals, apart from Anna Magnani and Aldo Fabrizi, and what Roberto shot was "guided by [his] own and the actors' moods and perspectives." The movie opened to mixed reviews in Italy in 1945 but was soon hailed by avant-garde directors such as Jean-Luc Godard as a masterpiece and is now regarded as one of the most influential films ever made. It became a box-office success in America after Rod Geiger launched a defamation case regarding his role in the supply of film, resulting in countless column inches of free publicity.

RIGHT
"I didn't want it to end," Ingrid said of Rome, Open City.

named Roberto Rossellini, and immediately recognized that the man was a genius. Later, she would say watching that film—the consequences that came of it—was the most important event of her life. She watched another of Roberto's movies, *Paisà* (1946), and then she wrote to him: "If you need a Swedish actress who speaks English very well, who has not forgotten her German, who is not very understandable in French, and who in Italian knows only *'ti amo,'* I am ready to come and make a film with you." When he received the letter, at first he didn't know who she was, but then he remembered seeing her in the Swedish version of *Intermezzo* during the war when he had rushed into a movie theater to shelter from a bombing raid. He arranged to meet Ingrid and Petter in Paris to discuss making a movie with her. None of their lives would ever be the same again.

A LOVABLE ROGUE

Just as Ingrid's childhood was overshadowed by bereavement, Roberto's had been constantly

interrupted by illness. He had bouts of malaria, cholera, pleurisy, and appendicitis, but the most life-threatening of all was when he contracted the severe influenza that swept the globe in 1918–20 and is estimated to have killed between 50 and 100 million people. For three months, Roberto's life hung in the balance and he had to have part of a lung removed, but in time he pulled through. So much of his childhood was spent bedridden that he developed a kind of devil-may-care attitude in his late teens. He liked fast cars, motorcycles, and sex, and he was prepared to take chances in life and embark on adventures. Film was in his blood because his father was an architect who designed several movie theaters in Rome, and they frequently watched movies together, so he always knew what he wanted to do in his future career.

He liked fast cars, motorcycles, and sex, and he was prepared to take chances in life and embark on adventures

As well as film, Roberto loved women and was very successful with them from his teenage years onward. Part of the secret of his success, according to his friend Federico Fellini, was that he was fascinated by them, and when a woman was with him she got his full attention. In 1931, he fell for a Russian comedienne called Assia Noris but she refused to sleep with him outside marriage. Undaunted, Roberto organized a big church wedding, complete with an archbishop, priests, and full festivities. After a year of marriage, the relationship failed and she asked him for a divorce. It was only then he confessed that the whole wedding had been stage-managed, with actors playing the religious figures.

His first proper marriage was to a costume designer called Marcella de Marchis in September 1936. They had two sons, Romano and Renzo, and Roberto's heart was broken when Romano died at the age of nine after succumbing to infection following an appendectomy. For the rest of his life, Roberto carried one of his son's tiny gloves in his wallet. He remained married to Marcella for fourteen years but had mistresses all over town, including the volatile actress Anna Magnani, who marked the end of their affair by tipping a bowl of spaghetti over his head in a restaurant. When asked by one former lover how he managed to juggle all his various affairs and marriages, he replied, "I always keep a window open."

When Roberto met Ingrid, he had already made seven feature films and established himself as a much-lauded creative director working in

the Italian neorealist style, along with his sometime collaborators
Fellini and Aldo Fabrizi. In his quest for realism he liked working with
non-professional actors and inviting them to improvise, and his movies,
particularly the two Ingrid had seen, were hugely influential. *Paisà* won
the New York Film Critics Award for Best Foreign Film in January 1949
and Roberto flew to New York to collect the award, then traveled on
to Hollywood to raise finance for a new film, *Stromboli*, that he wished
to make with Ingrid. He stayed in Ingrid and Petter's home and as
she showed him around LA, Roberto was knocked out by her beauty:
"Her smile lit up southern California, which was already a bright, sunny
place," he said. "She wasn't like other people there. She wasn't like
anybody anywhere." Her early impressions of him were also favorable:
"I was fascinated by him with my ears rather than with my eyes," she
explained. "He was a nice-looking man . . . But it was what he said rather
than what I saw that caused me to want to know him better."

She arrived in Rome on March 20, 1949, to start work on *Stromboli*,
and within days they were lovers. On April 3 she wrote to Petter telling
him of her infidelity. She hated causing pain to him and to her daughter
Pia, but her feelings for Roberto were overwhelming and quite
unstoppable. She didn't realize then that it would be seven years
before she saw Pia again.

BELOW
*"In the beginning, I
thought Roberto and
I were very much alike,"
said Ingrid. "[But] our
attraction was more of
opposites than of likes."*

A TURBULENT MARRIAGE

No one could have predicted the scale of the outrage caused by Ingrid and Roberto's affair. The Lutheran Church in Sweden and the Catholic Church in Rome both condemned her and she received sacks of hate mail from members of the public, mostly Americans. Some said she was an agent of the devil and would burn in hell for eternity; others called her a whore and a slut, and told her that the child she was expecting would be deformed or born dead. In March 1950, US senator Edwin C. Johnson of Colorado suggested they should pass a bill that would protect Americans from the "moral turpitude" of aliens such as Ingrid Bergman. Roberto told her to pay no attention and not to read the letters but she kept opening every one, hoping in vain to find at least one person who understood and sympathized.

Meanwhile, Petter was incandescent with rage and determined to obstruct his wife's affair in whatever way he could. He refused to give her a divorce in time for her to marry Roberto before their son was born. This meant that under Italian law, Ingrid's name could not appear on the birth certificate or Petter would have been assumed to be the father and would have the right to custody. He was already making it impossible for Pia to see her mother. When the new baby, whom they named Robertino, was born in a Rome hospital in February 1950, photographers tried to bribe the nuns to let them get a photograph of Ingrid with her "love child." One photographer checked his wife into the same hospital, forcing Ingrid and Roberto to escape in the middle of the night. It was May 1950 when she finally obtained a divorce from Petter in Mexico on the grounds of her "cruelty and desertion." Roberto divorced Marcella at the same time and they married in a Rome church, but if they thought things would be smooth sailing from there on, they were mistaken.

Professionally, they found it difficult to work with each other. Ingrid was used to being sent a script and turning up on set with all her lines learned and preparations made. Every camera angle and prop had been worked out in advance. Instead, she found that "With Roberto . . . there was nothing set, except in

> "I had rapturous happiness. I shed an ocean of tears. He wasn't ever boring"

ABOVE
Ingrid and Roberto after his return from India in 1957. "After what we had gone through to get married, it wasn't easy to admit to the world that it wasn't a perfect success," she said.

his mind, and that was, as I used to say, just a skeleton of a plan." Ingrid felt awkward when he asked her to improvise, especially since she still did not speak much Italian. After completing five movies with him, none of which was very successful, she asked if she might work with other directors, as she was still getting offers, but Roberto refused. "I think he would have preferred me to say I wanted to sleep with other directors," she joked later. "Perhaps he would have been more likely to say yes." She felt she needed to work because their financial situation was dire. Roberto insisted on living beyond their means and reacted with fury when she suggested they rein in their spending. His mother had always kept an "open table," feeding anyone who happened to be there at mealtimes, and he liked to be similarly generous. He felt an artist shouldn't even have to think about money and declared, "One should never regret spending money which brought pleasure." The financial crisis became even more acute after they had twin daughters, Isabella and Isotta, in 1952. If Roberto had made a successful movie in those years, Ingrid later speculated, it would have helped their marriage. He found it difficult that his wife was the sought-after commodity, while his work didn't achieve box-office success, and gradually the rifts began to appear.

"[The marriage] was up and down," Ingrid recalled in her autobiography. "I had rapturous happiness. I shed an ocean of tears. He wasn't ever boring." But the writing was on the wall when she went to make a picture with Jean Renoir in Paris in 1956 against Roberto's wishes, then another Hollywood picture, *Anastasia*, for which she would win an Oscar. When Roberto flew out to India to make a documentary about the country at the invitation of Prime Minister Nehru, Ingrid still clung to the hope that their marriage would last for life and was devastated when rumors filtered back that he was having an affair with a screenwriter, Sonali Das Gupta. Sonali was married and it led to a scandal in India every bit as frenzied as the one his affair with Ingrid had caused in America. The marriage that had seemed such a perfect love match was over within just seven years.

THE LAST DINNER & LUNCH

Roberto married Sonali, but was not faithful to her. Ingrid married a Swedish theater producer named Lars Schmidt but the marriage foundered because of the amount of time she spent away from home making movies. Relations between Ingrid and Roberto were strained for a while, with him forbidding her from taking his children to America and trying to insist that Ingrid would never remarry. However, as time passed they became friends and Pia and her half-siblings met and got along with each other.

One night in spring 1977 Ingrid and Roberto found that by chance they were both staying at the Hotel Raphael in Paris and agreed to have dinner. She had been battling breast cancer since 1973 and he listened as she confided in him about her illness, her work, and their children. It went so well that they agreed to have lunch together the next day before going their separate ways. Ingrid had no idea it was the last time she would ever see him, but on June 3 he died of a massive heart attack. In his last minutes, it was his first wife, Marcella, he telephoned. She lived across the street and was able to rush over and hold him in her arms as he passed away. "It was like a part of me had died," Ingrid said. "It was at that moment I knew how much I still loved him. . . . I knew I would miss Roberto every day as long as I lived." Their love hadn't lasted but despite its brevity, it was precious and profoundly life-enhancing.

BELOW
Roberto and Ingrid, 1953. His friend, director Federico Fellini, said, "Women loved [him]. I didn't understand then what this fascination he had was, but now I think I do. It was because he was fascinated by them."

FRANK SINATRA
&
AVA GARDNER

FRANCIS ALBERT SINATRA

BORN: DECEMBER 12, 1915
HOBOKEN, NEW JERSEY

DIED: MAY 14, 1998
WEST HOLLYWOOD, CALIFORNIA

AVA LAVINIA GARDNER

BORN: DECEMBER 24, 1922
SMITHFIELD, NORTH CAROLINA

DIED: JANUARY 25, 1990
LONDON, ENGLAND

MARRIED: NOVEMBER 7, 1951
GERMANTOWN, PENNSYLVANIA

RIGHT
Frank and Ava out on the town and (inset) on their wedding day, for which she wore a dress of mauve marquisette with a pink taffeta top.

He was a self-confessed "18-karat manic depressive" and she was a hard-drinking sex addict who couldn't bear to be alone.

On their second date, Frank and Ava drove into the desert, drunk as skunks, and shot out the streetlights in a small town called Indio with his Smith & Wesson handgun, before getting arrested. It was a foretaste of the relationship ahead: dangerous, destructive, compulsive, and utterly insane.

*B*oth Frank and Ava had their problems when they got together. He was a self-confessed "18-karat manic depressive" and she was a hard-drinking sex addict who couldn't bear to be alone. It was a recipe for disaster but they were irresistibly drawn to each other like moths to a flame.

Frank's birth was traumatic. He was a 13-pound baby born to a mother who was only 5 feet tall, so the doctor had to yank him out with forceps that scarred his cheek and neck. The baby wasn't breathing so he was put to one side while everyone tended to his mother, Dolly, and it was only because a grandmother held him under the cold tap that Frank took his first breath. His parents were immigrants—his father from Sicily, his mother from Genoa—and he grew up in an Italian neighborhood in Hoboken, New Jersey, where he hung out with "tough kids on street corners" and witnessed gang fights. His father was a ship's boilermaker, a boxer, then a fireman, and his mother was a midwife and sometime abortionist (nicknamed Hatpin Dolly), who was deeply involved in local politics. Young Frank got into a few scrapes, stealing bicycles and the like, but once he discovered music, in particular his idol Bing Crosby, he knew what he wanted to do with his life.

Dolly called on local Italian business owners to give her boy a chance, and as a teenager he began playing at beer parties and roadhouses, with a repertoire that included the works of some of the great songwriters of the day: Cole Porter, Irving Berlin, and George Gershwin. His first serious girlfriend was local girl Nancy Rose Barbato, whom he started dating when he was twenty and she seventeen, and in February 1939 he married her at Our Lady of the Sorrow Church in Jersey City. On their wedding day, he gave her a romantic record he'd made especially for her entitled "Our Love"—but he wasn't ever faithful to her. In February 1938 he was arrested for "seduction and adultery" after sleeping with a local woman, and he was always happy to have backstage tumbles with fans who pursued him, so long as they were pretty enough. Nancy learned to turn away when he came home smelling of another woman. Frank was a good Catholic boy and all she

Frank and Nancy with their children Frank, Jr, Tina (on her mom's knee), and Nancy, Jr. Frank was obsessed with cleanliness and took up to twelve showers a day—probably to wash off the scent of other women.

could hope was that he would always return to her, especially after the children were born in 1940, 1944, and 1948.

A turning point came when Frank got a contract with the Tommy Dorsey Band, and quickly won popularity with his mixture of intimate crooning and impeccable pitch and timing. You could feel the emotion, the personality, in each and every number. He broke away from Dorsey to go solo, and the fans besieged him after every show. In 1941, he applied for war service but was turned down because of a perforated eardrum and because the examiners found him "neurotic." Instead, he spent the war years developing what became known as "The Voice," and in 1944 when Hollywood called, he uprooted the family and relocated to the West Coast. He signed with MGM and made *Anchors Aweigh* (1945) with Gene Kelly, the first of many musicals in which he appeared. There were gorgeous actresses everywhere and Frank had affairs with Marlene Dietrich and Lana Turner, to name but two. A pianist, Skitch Henderson, introduced him to Ava Gardner, who at the time was married to Mickey Rooney, the pint-sized star of the popular *Andy Hardy* series. "Why didn't I meet you first?" he flirted, his pale blue eyes sparkling as he checked out her curves. Years later, long after she'd broken up with Rooney, they ran into each other in the street and went for dinner, but although she was attracted to him she refused to go to bed with a married man. All would have been well, perhaps, if his pal Peter Lawford hadn't brought her along to a party one night in Palm Springs, where that same evening Frank and Ava drove off into the desert and shot out the streetlights in Indio. Studio publicists had to bribe the local authorities with a big check to get them out of jail without charges being pressed. The romance was on, and it was already trouble with a capital T.

BIRTH OF A SEX GODDESS

Ava was born to tobacco and cotton farming folk in Smithfield, North Carolina, with a mixture of French, Scots, Irish, English, and Native

American ancestry. She was the youngest of seven kids and close to an older sister, Beatrice, whom she called "Bappie." Ava always loved the movies, and it was through Bappie's husband, a New York photographer, that she would get her first chance on the silver screen. She was just seventeen and extraordinarily beautiful when he stuck a photograph of her in his shop window, where it attracted the attention of a talent scout. A batch of pictures was sent to MGM's New York office and Ava was invited for a screen test. It was something of a disaster because she was terribly self-conscious and her thick Southern accent was virtually indecipherable, but when Louis B. Mayer saw it, he sent a telegram that read, "She can't sing, she can't act, she can't talk. She's terrific!" Ava and Bappie headed out to the West Coast and her training began. First a speech coach worked on changing her accent into middle American, then an acting coach took over. Meanwhile, Mickey Rooney had spotted her in the corridors and was instantly smitten. "Everything in me stopped," he wrote in his autobiography. "My heart. My breathing. My thinking." He pursued her relentlessly, and when she agreed to dinner, he proposed marriage on the first date. Persistence paid off and after he'd asked her to marry him twenty-five times, she finally said yes.

On their wedding night, January 10, 1942, Mickey found that nineteen-year-old Ava was a virgin. Her Baptist upbringing had given her a fear of the mechanics of sex and of getting a bad reputation, but once initiated she discovered that she loved it. Mickey was the happy beneficiary as she experimented and developed her own techniques, but out of bed they began to argue constantly and she walked out in 1943, leaving him heartbroken. She began a dalliance with Howard Hughes, the multi-millionaire owner of RKO Studios, and kept him hooked for several years without ever sleeping with him. His wealth and power were fascinating to her but she didn't find him attractive and she was

BELOW
When they met, Mickey Rooney was a huge star, most famous for the series of movies featuring the teenaged character Andy Hardy, while Ava was an ingénue—but she didn't stay naive for long.

" *Everything in me stopped ... My heart. My breathing. My thinking* "

CONFIDENTIAL MAGAZINE

In 1952, a brand new magazine was launched with the express goal of spreading scandal about the stars. Its writers got their information from a network of waitresses, starlets, and call girls, and the new technology of miniature cameras and listening devices made their job easier. Informants were paid for scoops, so some journalists, including gossip columnist Walter Winchell, gave stories to *Confidential* that they couldn't publish in the respectable press. Any old fact could be woven into an article with a bit of embellishment here and there, and usually the stars concerned didn't sue as that would only draw attention to the story. *Confidential*'s "scoops" included alleging Bing Crosby beat his wife, and that Rock Hudson and Liberace were gay. Ava Gardner's lifestyle and lovers were a rich source of material and she was featured in most issues. The readership was huge, topping four million by the second issue. As Humphrey Bogart said, "Everybody reads it but they say the cook brought it into the house." Its decline began when it lost a string of lawsuits in the late 1950s and in 1978 it closed down.

spooked when she found out that he had her under 24-hour surveillance, checking who she was seeing and what time she got home at night. When he tried to make a move on her, she swung at him and left him requiring stitches to his face, but still he was obsessed with her.

Her second marriage was to band-leader Artie Shaw and this was quite a different affair. He was an intellectual who gave her reading lists to try to educate her and scoffed at her "hick" background. When she kicked off her shoes to tuck her bare feet beneath her on a chair, he snapped, "For god's sake, what are you doing? Do you think you're still in a tobacco field?" He played on her insecurities about her background and her lack of talent, and when he left her she was bereft. "I don't trust love any more," she told a friend. "It led me astray."

Fortunately, Artie's departure coincided with her first decent film role, as a femme fatale in *The Killers* (1946). The posters featured her, larger than life, in a skin-tight black satin dress, and many of the rave reviews praised her in particular. Up to then, she'd

just been playing bit parts, but now she proved she could handle a lead role, and more followed in *The Hucksters* (1947) and *The Great Sinner* (1949), both of them portraying her as a temptress. It was typecasting, because that's what Ava had become. Free of marital commitments, she hit the town running, and was soon partying all night, drinking heavily, and having affairs with all and sundry: Clark Gable, David Niven, Kirk Douglas, Robert Taylor, Robert Mitchum, and plenty more. There were rumors of group sex, visits to brothels, and S&M sessions. All those early fears about getting a bad reputation flew out the window. She was beautiful, exciting—and completely off the rails.

She was beautiful, exciting—and completely off the rails

ABOVE
With Robert Mitchum
in My Forbidden Past
(1951). She wrote in her
memoirs, "If I could have
gotten him into bed,
I would have." And he
retorted, "She could
get him into bed, and
she did."

SCANDAL ERUPTS

Ava had told Frank she wouldn't have an affair with him because he was married, but after the night they were arrested together in 1949, she changed her mind. Frank told her his marriage with Nancy was over and that they didn't have sex any more, which she believed, despite the fact they'd had a daughter just the year before. After their first night together, Ava wrote "I truly felt that no matter what happened we would always be in love." They fell into a passionate, tempestuous affair, and although they tried to keep it quiet, the gossip columnists were soon onto them and the furor was monumental. Readers were

LEFT
With Gregory Peck
in The Snows of
Kilimanjaro, 1952.
He said, "I've always
admired her as an
actress and felt she
was underrated because
people were deceived by
her beauty and did not
expect more from her."

incensed and most of their fury was directed at Ava. Letters poured
into the studios accusing her of being a witch, a tramp, and a Jezebel,
and expressing their support for poor innocent Nancy, the faithful wife
and mother back home. Roman Catholic priests and nuns were critical
of Sinatra, and he even got a letter from New Jersey Mafia boss Willie
Moretti expressing his "surprise" about the marriage breakup. Frank got
into a few scuffles with photographers, which didn't help one bit, then
he punched gossip columnist Lee Mortimer in Ciro's nightclub. But he
never considered going back to Nancy. He was obsessed with Ava and
would have done anything for her. Anything at all.

Ava was crazy about Frank, too. Like her, he had his insecurities. He
was also from a poor, working-class background and sensitive to those
who looked down on him for his lack of education. Like her, he was
restless and easily bored. She knew his reputation and became jealous
of any other woman his glance so much as flickered over. Fights flared
up in which furniture was knocked over and insults screamed, then they

RIGHT
In 1951, Frank co-wrote
the song "I'm a Fool to
Want You" about Ava.
It was his first recording
with new label Capitol
Records and helped to
revive his singing career
in the 1950s.

rushed to bed to make up. "Frankie and I are both high-strung people," she told a columnist. "Possessive, jealous, and liable to explode fast." But she was the one who was unfaithful first, when she filmed *Pandora and the Flying Dutchman* in Spain in spring 1951 and ended up in bed with a bullfighter, Mario Cabre. Frank flew over, the truth came out, and he was apoplectic with rage, but he should have known better than to leave Ava alone for four months. She never could bear to sleep alone.

> " They were both possessive, jealous, and liable to explode fast "

Meanwhile, Frank's career was on the rocks: he had been fired by MGM (supposedly for a joke he told about Louis B. Mayer but probably also because they saw him as difficult) and was singing three shows a night at the Copacabana in New York, which put a strain on his voice. Nancy took a third of his income plus the family home in the separation agreement but refused to give him a divorce—she was certain that the affair would burn out and he'd be home before long. In the face of all this pressure, Frank took an overdose of phenobarbital, a sedative, and Ava rushed to his side, but he hadn't taken enough to do any lasting harm. Nancy finally divorced him on October 30, 1951, and Ava and Frank were married just eight days later. The press got word of the location and once again Frank had a run-in with photographers. There was just time for a quick honeymoon in Miami and Havana before work commitments took them to opposite sides of the Atlantic again.

"A LIGHTED MATCH TO TNT"

Separation was the worst possible thing for a volatile couple like Frank and Ava. In Africa on location for the movie *Mogambo* (1953) she found she was pregnant and flew to London to have the baby aborted without telling him. When he found out, he was heartbroken. She had said she wanted to have a family with him, so he couldn't understand why she didn't keep the baby. Gossips speculated that maybe it wasn't his.

Frank's career picked up in 1953 when he got a role in the eve-of-Pearl-Harbor movie *From Here to Eternity*, but his relationship was heading downhill fast. On October 29 that year, his separation from Ava was announced in the press. Later she would blame his infidelities and say, "If I'd been willing to share him with other women, we could have been happy." His friends said she had become unreasonable and demanding, and that her constant alcoholic haranguing had something to do with the split as well. Frank thought it was a temporary

separation, but she quickly sought solace with another bullfighter, Luis Miguel Dominguín, leaving Humphrey Bogart, Sinatra's drinking buddy, mystified. "Half the world's female population would throw themselves at Frank's feet and here you are flouncing around with guys who wear capes and little ballerina slippers," he said. Gradually it dawned on Frank that Ava wasn't coming back and he went berserk. When his friend Peter Lawford took her out for a drink, he threatened to break Peter's legs. He cut his wrists one night in an apparent suicide attempt and was rushed to hospital, and he ranted and raved about Ava to anyone who would listen. As one friend commented wearily, "A billion broads in the world and he picks the one that can take or leave him!"

There were several reunions, including one when he flew all the way to Australia just to see her, but they always ended up fighting Utterly worn out, they divorced in 1957, but emotionally they couldn't get over each other. She still loved him, but she knew that they were too explosive together. As a friend said, it was like "bringing a lighted match to TNT." From a distance she eulogized Frank—he became her knight in shining armor, the one she could always depend on—and she never found another lover to take his place, although there would be dozens more men in her life. She had bitter regrets about their breakup but she also believed it couldn't have been any other way.

They spoke on the telephone over the next few decades and were friends of sorts, but when Ava heard Frank had married Mia Farrow in

July 1966 she burst into tears and couldn't stop crying. That marriage was over within a couple of years, and a decade later he married Las Vegas showgirl Barbara Marx—but still he brooded about Ava. His career was stratospheric, with hit records, awards galore, and his legendary Las Vegas shows. Ava's career was not in such good shape; after *The Night of the Iguana* (1964), based on a Tennessee Williams play and starring Richard Burton and Deborah Kerr, then *Mayerling* (1968), in which she played an Austrian Empress, she was mainly offered B-movie roles and TV miniseries.

During the last year of her life, when Ava was living in London and struggling with emphysema after a lifetime of heavy smoking, Frank flew her out to America on a private plane to see a specialist. And when news reached him that she had died, his eyes filled with tears and, according to his daughter Nancy, he sat alone in his room all night and all the following day. As well as those two later marriages, Frank had dozens more affairs, but Ava remained special. They had loved each other heart and soul but their feelings were too intense and ultimately they were both too unstable to be able to make it work.

MAFIA CONNECTIONS

Frank Sinatra was dogged by rumors of Mafia connections, and he admitted he knew some of the Dons of the day because of the New Jersey society in which he had grown up. But when he flew to Havana in 1947 and sang for a conference of the country's top mobsters, including Lucky Luciano and Meyer Lansky, he was pushing his luck. In December 1950 he was called in front of a Senate committee to account for his "friendship" with these men, and he nervously and somewhat unconvincingly said that he had bumped into them but had no idea who they were or what they did. In 1953, some speculated that his Mafia connections had helped him to win the role in *From Here to Eternity* that revived his career and won him an Oscar. Such a scenario is dramatized in Mario Puzo's novel *The Godfather*, but the truth is that Frank lobbied hard for the part and offered to waive his fee, so there may not have been anything sinister about it. However, he was known for frequently issuing threats to have people beaten up or killed whenever they annoyed him, which didn't help to quell rumors of his links to the mob.

YVES MONTAND

&

SIMONE SIGNORET

IVO LIVI

BORN: OCTOBER 13, 1921
MONSUMMANO TERME, ITALY

DIED: NOVEMBER 9, 1991
MONSUMMANO, ITALY

SIMONE HENRIETTE
CHARLOTTE KAMINKER

BORN: MARCH 25, 1921
WIESBADEN, GERMANY

DIED: SEPTEMBER 30, 1985
AUTHEUIL-AUTHOUILLET, FRANCE

★

MARRIED: DECEMBER 22, 1951
ST-PAUL-DE-VENCE, FRANCE

RIGHT
*Yves loved to make
Simone laugh. "If you
don't laugh together
on a film, you will
never be able to
make people cry
together," she wrote
in her autobiography.*

"*We had been struck by lightning, and something indiscreet and irreversible had happened*"

ABOVE AND RIGHT
Yves (above) was a little in awe of Simone (right), who was described by friends as "much more harsh, more violent, than he." Yet at home, she let him be the dictator. "Once in a while a man has to tell his wife to wash his socks," he said.

"It was a wonderful day," said Yves of his first meeting with Simone. "I'll never get tired of going over the details with my magnifying glass—her blonde hair, the burning sun, and the exact moment when [she] watched me coming toward her."

They met on August 19, 1949, in a courtyard of the Colombe d'Or hotel in St-Paul-De-Vence on France's Côte d'Azur. Yves was there to have dinner with his guitarist, Henri Crolla, and his pianist, Bob Castella. Simone was with movie director Jacques Prévert, who knew Crolla from the Café de Flore in Paris, where they both hung out. There were introductions all around, although Yves knew Simone's face from the cover of magazines. She was obviously smart and intellectual, but he made her laugh by playing the fool, one of his Don Juan techniques developed over many years of practice. He knew she was married and had a three-year-old daughter, but he invited her to his concert in Cannes the following evening, then she invited him back to the small house she owned by the church in St-Paul-De-Vence. They had just four days together before he had to leave but, as Simone recalled, "We had been struck by lightning, and something indiscreet and irreversible had happened."

"It was a great love," Montand said in his memoirs. "In the early days it was *l'amour fou*. Crazy!" He couldn't bear to be without her and gave her an ultimatum: she must come and live with him or it was over. And so she moved into his tiny two-bedroom flat in Neuilly, on the outskirts of Paris, leaving her daughter behind at first, and ignoring the signs of all the other women who had passed through his bedroom over the years. That is how their great, life-changing passion began.

BELOW
Simone gently steered Yves toward career choices she thought would be good for him.

THE CAFÉ DE FLORE

Simone's father, André Kaminker, was a Polish Jew, and she was born in the Rhineland where he served in the army of Occupation after World War I. The family lived in a house requisitioned from its German owners, who were sheltering in the attic. Simone's mother felt sorry for them and made sure they got enough milk for their children, because food shortages were rife for Germans. In 1923,

CARNÉ & PRÉVERT

Screenwriter and poet Jacques Prévert and film director Marcel Carné were the power duo of French cinema in the 1930s and 1940s, working together on dozens of movies, most famously *Les Enfants du Paradis* (1945), which many critics consider to be one of the greats of all time. They were part of the poetic realism movement, which aimed to reflect the grittier side of life in a stylized rather than a documentary fashion, and which tended to reflect left-wing sensibilities. Think ladies of the night, petty criminals, and army deserters battling to stay alive in rain-soaked, run-down neighborhoods. During the German Occupation of France, Prévert and Carné continued to work despite difficult conditions as the Nazis instructed them to make "escapist" movies, imposed a curfew, and stood guard on set. Still they managed to employ two Jewish crew members and finish filming *Les Enfants* around the time of the American landings on the south coast of France in August 1944. Simone Signoret first worked with Carné in 1942 on *Le Voyageur de la Toussaint*, and in 1943 she appeared in Prévert's *Adieu Léonard*. Yves Montand made his movie debut in their final collaboration, *Les Portes de la Nuit*, in 1946.

the Kaminkers moved back to France and lived in the middle-class suburb of Neuilly, where André got a job in advertising, then worked as a translator, famously translating during the 1938 negotiations between Hitler and Édouard Daladier, which everyone hoped would prevent another war. They didn't, of course, and André fled to London, leaving his family in wartime France. Simone adopted her mother's maiden name, Signoret—Kaminker sounded too Jewish—and took a job at a right-wing newspaper called *Les Nouveaux Temps*, until she realized the staff were collaborating with the Germans, whereupon she left.

Simone had always wanted to be an actress, and one evening in spring 1941, when she was twenty years old, a friend took her along to the Café de Flore, home away from home for Paris's left-wing intellectuals, and rightaway she was hooked. They talked about philosophy, art, cinema, and politics, and she drank it in, making some of the most important friendships of her life. She met people who worked in movies, including Jacques Prévert and screenwriter Marcel Carné, and began to get work as an extra (known in France as a *silhouette*). She also

LEFT
Jacques Prévert: his poems are widely taught in French schools but his screenplays for Marcel Carné are the work for which he still receives international acclaim.

worked in theater and had a few boyfriends
whom she met through the crowd at the Flore.
It was an exciting time, her only regret after
the war being that she had not actively worked
for the Resistance despite knowing many
people who had.

She had a style all
her own——a sense
of presence, a sense
of passion

Toward the war's end, she began an affair
with a married director, Yves Allégret, who
gave her her first speaking role in a movie
called *Les Démons de l'Aube*—and who
also gave her a child, Catherine, born in
1946. Motherhood didn't stop Simone in
her ambitions, though, and she played a
"girl of easy virtue" in *Macadam* (1946)
while still breastfeeding, then a prostitute
in *Dédée d'Anvers* (1948), the movie that
would make her name. According to the
Paris-Press reviewer, this film "immediately
raises her up with the first rank of French
screen actresses." She had a style all her
own—a sense of presence, a sense of
passion, and those extraordinary, twinkling

eyes. Her fame crossed the Atlantic and Howard Hughes, RKO
president, offered her a four-year contract to make a movie a year.
How could she refuse? Before sailing to the US, she went for a
well-earned rest in St-Paul-de-Vence—and met the man who would
turn her entire life upside down.

ABOVE
Simone in Manèges
*(1950), directed by her
then-husband Yves
Allégret. This dark,
slightly misogynistic
movie concerns a gold-
digging woman on
whom the tables
are turned.*

"IVO! MONTA!"

Ivo Livi was born in a tiny mountain village in Tuscany, where his father,
a confirmed Marxist, owned a broom factory. One night the factory
was burned down by supporters of the Fascist Prime Minister Benito
Mussolini and the family fled to Marseilles, where Ivo's father found
work in the docks. They were very poor, and Ivo later recalled, "Often
all we had for lunch was one egg for all three kids." Ivo left school at
eleven and worked in factories, at a hairdresser's, and as a riveter on
the docks. He dreamed of one day being in the movies and perfected
his imitations of Clark Gable, Humphrey Bogart, and Donald Duck
to entertain his workmates. He also sang, and entered a talent
competition at the age of seventeen. Although he sang off-key and

A tongue-in-cheek
feature for the magazine
L'Écran in which Yves
sings and plays piano
for his maid and his
cook. It was 1947, the
year after Edith Piaf
left him and two years
before he met Simone.

could not remember the words, he found that
he loved performing, and started singing at
local clubs, adopting the stage name Yves
Montand because it sounded like *"Ivo! Monta!"*
(Ivo! Climb!).

In early 1944, he received notice to report
for forced labor under the German Army of
Occupation, but instead he fled to Paris,
where he began singing American cowboy-style
ballads, which went down a storm with
Parisians who were longing to be liberated by
the Allies. In late May, he met Edith Piaf, the
"little sparrow" who filled the Moulin Rouge
every night with her huge, soulful voice. She
was looking for a singer to impersonate an
American star in her act, and fell for Yves'
charm. She taught him all she knew as a
performer, persuading him to give up
the American numbers and choose a
sophisticated Parisian repertoire with a suave stage style.
She was six years older than he was but, according to Yves, "she was
great fun . . . and very, very pretty." They became lovers and Yves
described her as *"formidable,"* adding, "She only knew how to give—
everything." But in 1946, when he had become almost as famous as her,
she left him overnight, without explanation. He was shattered and it
took him a while to put himself back together again, but meantime he
consoled himself in the arms of groupies who came backstage after his
concerts. And then, on a summer night when he was twenty-eight years
old, he met Simone and knew immediately that this was the real thing.

Through her, Yves met cultural icons—Picasso, Jean-Paul Sartre,
and Simone de Beauvoir—and they entertained frequently in their
small apartment in the Place Dauphine in Paris. He frequently made
Simone dissolve into giggles with his accurate impersonations and witty
observations. They were inseparable—he sat on the edge of the set
while she was filming, and she was in the wings at all his concerts. Yves
had recently signed a seven-year contract with Warner Brothers in
Hollywood, and they discussed going over together, but their left-wing
politics were at odds with the zeitgeist in the US. In 1950, they signed
the Stockholm Petition calling for a ban on all nuclear weapons, the act
of Communists in the view of the US authorities, who promptly

rescinded their entry visas. In fact, though they were not card-carrying Communists, their sympathies leaned very much in that direction until the invasion of Hungary in 1956 showed an ugly side to the Soviet regime that caused them to reassess their allegiance.

Meanwhile, their careers went from strength to strength. She made the acclaimed movies *Casque d'Or* (1952), *Thérèse Raquin* (1953), and *Les Diaboliques* (1954), while he wrote protest songs, interspersing them with conventional numbers in his set, and also began to act in films. They bought a country house at Autheuil in Normandy in which to relax, and tried to coordinate their work so that there were no long periods of separation. There was a balance of power in the relationship. Both had successful careers and respected each other's achievements. She was no feminist, though; at home she was a wife and he was the head of the household. That's the way they liked it.

LET'S MAKE LOVE

In 1959, America came calling again when Yves was offered a solo show on Broadway. The McCarthy Era now firmly in the past, they settled themselves in a New York apartment and his show soon became the

BELOW
"Chains do not hold a marriage together," Simone wrote. *"It is threads, hundreds of tiny threads which sew people together through the years."*

hottest ticket in town. One night playwright Arthur Miller came backstage with his wife Marilyn Monroe and introductions were made all around. Simone and Yves had appeared in a production of Miller's play *The Crucible*, which they greatly admired, and they shared the same left-of-center views. Marilyn needed a costar in the movie she was about to make, *Let's Make Love*, and suggested Yves. How could he refuse? In early 1960 the two couples moved into suites across the hall from each other in Hollywood's Beverly Wilshire Hotel and became friends, often dining together. Marilyn opened up to Simone about her insecurities, both physical and intellectual. Simone admired her honesty but thought of her as a kind of lost child, with Arthur as the long-suffering father figure trying to keep her on track.

Simone's career had been on the back burner during this period, but then they heard that she was nominated for the Best Actress Oscar for her role in *Room at the Top* (1959) as a middle-aged woman having an affair with a young man. She won, and when she went on stage to collect her statuette, she said, "I could see dear old Montand sobbing away as if he'd just buried his twelve best friends." The following day, she had to fly to Italy to start work on her next movie, leaving him behind.

The filming of *Let's Make Love* was delayed after a strike among the crew, and in mid-April 1960 Arthur Miller had to return to New York for some appointments, leaving Yves and Marilyn alone. Marilyn was jealous of Simone's Oscar and confided in Yves her fear that she would never be any good as an actress. Yves confessed that he suffered from

BELOW
Simone accepts her Best Actress Oscar from Rock Hudson in 1959. "I rushed to the platform, in tears, running like a madwoman," she told a journalist. "Goodbye cool head and self-control."

stage fright before every single performance, and that he was particularly nervous about making a movie in English because he understood so little of the language. And then, according to legend, Marilyn appeared in his room one night wearing a fur coat and nothing underneath. "What am I to do?" Yves asked later. "I cannot alienate her because I depend on her good will and I wish to work with her. I am truly in a trap." Their affair began around late April 1960 and the story hit the newsstands almost immediately.

Back in Europe, journalists asked Simone for her reaction to her husband's infidelity. She hid her true emotions and answered, "You know many men, do you, who would have stayed indifferent while having Marilyn Monroe in their arms?" Yves soon found that the affair was a poisoned chalice, with Marilyn desperately seeking someone on whom to offload her angst and neediness as her marriage to Miller reached its death throes. After filming finished at the end of June 1960, Yves broke up with her in a Cadillac on his way to the airport and was surprised by the heartbroken reaction. Marilyn had thought he would leave Simone for her, and he assured her that "not for a moment" had that been a possibility. He loved his wife too much. He had misjudged Marilyn, he realized—"I was wrong to believe that she was as sophisticated as certain other ladies I have known."

Yves got home to find Simone badly wounded by the affair. "I pay a lot after that," he said later. "Oh brother!" It wasn't the mere fact of his betrayal, but the very public nature of it, with a woman five years her junior who was the universal symbol of sexiness. At that moment something deep within Simone had changed and she would never be quite the same again.

TILL DEATH DO US PART

Forty is a sensitive age for an actress. Wrinkles are appearing, the jawline is dropping, and the parts being offered are character roles rather than romantic leads. Around that time Simone stopped caring about her appearance quite so much. What's the point when one's

ABOVE
"Next to my husband and Marlon Brando, I think Yves Montand is the most attractive man I've ever met," Marilyn announced as filming began on Let's Make Love.

— 149 —

husband runs off with a sex goddess anyway? She started drinking
more than was good for her and threw herself into her career and into
politics. She translated Lillian Hellmann's play *The Little Foxes* for the
French stage in 1962, and starred in it; she received another Oscar
nomination for playing a morphine-addicted Contessa in *Ship of Fools*
(1965); and she campaigned vehemently against injustice wherever she
saw it. There was still tenderness and understanding between her and
Yves but the passion had cooled, and following his tryst with Marilyn he
began to stray elsewhere. "Simone was very wise," he said.
"I will not say she closed her eyes but at least she lowered
her lids." He was sad about her drinking and sad that she let
herself go—"I told her it's not fair for her and it's not fair for
me"—but there was nothing he could do.

> "*I will not say
she closed her eyes
but at least she
lowered her lids.*"

In the 1970s, Simone turned to writing, something she had
always wanted to try, and her memoirs, *Nostalgia Isn't What It
Used To Be*, were published in 1976 to great acclaim. In them,
she gave her reaction to the affair with Marilyn, who was now
long dead: "She will never know how much I *didn't* hate her."
She described a champagne-colored silk scarf Marilyn had once given
her: "It's a bit frayed by now, but if you fold it in the right way, you don't
notice." Simone stopped drinking in the late 1970s but ill health caught
up with her anyway. She had an operation to remove her gall bladder
in 1980, and her eyesight began to fail, gradually at first and then more
rapidly. Still she managed to write a novel, *Adieu Volodya* (1985), and
she played a role in a television drama when almost completely blind.
What she missed most, she told a biographer, was being able to catch

eyes with Yves across the dinner table and know without words exactly what he was thinking. In 1985 she was diagnosed with pancreatic cancer and died, aged sixty-four, in their house in Autheuil. Yves was in the middle of filming *Jean de Florette* (1986) and had to return, greatly upset, to finish the movie after her funeral. His role as the scheming farmer in this and its sequel *Manon des Sources* (1986) would bring him late-career accolades, but it must have been difficult to carry on after losing the great love of his life.

In the final six years of his own life, Yves married a girl named Carole Amiel who had been his assistant on a world tour and was forty years younger than he was. They had a child, Valentin, something he had never done with Simone. He died on the set of *IPS: The Island of Pachyderms* (1992) on the very last day of filming after his very last retakes. The movie tells of an old man who dies of a heart attack, and Yves did exactly the same thing. There was no question but that he would be buried alongside Simone in Paris's Père Lachaise cemetery. It was the memory of her strength that had kept him working, kept him going, right up till the end.

POLITICALLY ACTIVE ACTORS

There has long been a trend for political activism in the arts in France, perhaps since the Revolution taught citizens to strive for *Liberté, Egalité,* and *Fraternité,* and Simone Signoret and Yves Montand were not unusual as artists in having a strident left-wing agenda. In America, actors were seen as entertainers pure and simple and few involved themselves openly in political affairs until the Hollywood Ten, a group of screenwriters and directors, were blacklisted in 1947 for alleged Communist sympathies. Charlie Chaplin and Orson Welles were among those who left America in protest at the Communist witch hunt; Chaplin found he was banned from re-entering the country, while Paul Robeson had his passport rescinded. In the late 1950s after the discrediting of the House Un-American Activities Committee, which had been set up to investigate "subversive activities," there was a push to redress any wrongs, and some suspected that Simone Signoret's 1959 Best Actress Oscar was motivated partly by a desire on the part of the judges to show a return to free expression.

ARTHUR
MILLER
&
MARILYN
MONROE

ARTHUR ASHER MILLER

BORN: OCTOBER 17, 1915
NEW YORK CITY

DIED: FEBRUARY 10, 2005
ROXBURY, CONNECTICUT

NORMA JEANE MORTENSON

BORN: JUNE 1, 1926
LOS ANGELES, CALIFORNIA

DIED: AUGUST 5, 1962
LOS ANGELES, CALIFORNIA

★

MARRIED: JUNE 29, 1956
WHITE PLAINS, NEW YORK

RIGHT
Newlyweds Arthur and Marilyn in England in summer 1956 when she was filming The Prince and The Showgirl. *Inset: an infamous shot from* The Seven Year Itch *(1955).*

ABOVE
On the set of Some Like It Hot
(1959). Arthur tried to mediate
between Marilyn and director
Billy Wilder, and defended her
when Wilder publicly attacked
her for a lack of professionalism.

The unlikely match between the Hollywood sex bomb and the Pulitzer-Prize-winning playwright was the stuff of legend and generated countless newspaper headlines around the globe. But it was doomed to failure because neither would ever be able to find what they had been seeking in the other.

*M*ental illness is sometimes caused by genetics and sometimes by a succession of tragic and difficult life events. In Marilyn Monroe's case, there were umpteen predisposing factors: a mother who spent much of her adult life in an insane asylum and several other close relatives who suffered from fragile mental health; being shunted around to different homes and guardians as a child; suffering abuse at the hands of men she hoped would help her as she tried to establish herself in Hollywood; serious problems with her physical health; numerous miscarriages and abortions; an addiction to prescription pills and booze; and the fact that the men she fell in love with always left her. That's just for starters. That she rose from this troubled background to become such a successful actress and global icon speaks volumes for her underlying determination to succeed. But she would not be so lucky in her main quest—to find love.

Norma Jeane's mother, Gladys, had two broken marriages and already had two children, who were being brought up by an ex-husband's family, when she got pregnant as a result of a fling with a philanderer named Stanley Gifford. He disappeared, and Norma Jeane was born illegitimate to a mentally ill woman who was completely incapable of looking after her. She was taken in by a religious couple, the Bolenders, who cared for her till the age of seven. There was a brief period when she lived with her mother, during which she witnessed Gladys having several terrifying manic episodes. At the age of nine, Norma Jeane was admitted to an orphanage for a couple of years and was then shuttled between a succession of foster homes. It was

BELOW
With her mother, Gladys, on the beach. Gladys worked for a while as a film cutter in a lab and loved to gossip about the stars, little dreaming that her daughter would one day be the biggest of them all.

> *She had an undulating walk that made her derrière look like "two puppies fighting under a sheet"*

no surprise at all that she fell into marriage with a neighbor's son, Jimmy Dougherty, at the age of sixteen. She yearned for a stable home life and this handsome, athletic boy seemed to offer it— but he went off to war in spring 1944 and came back to find his wife had changed. She had been "discovered" by a photographer and started a modeling career, which led to some bit parts in Hollywood movies. Fiercely ambitious, Norma Jeane slept with anyone she thought could help her on the path to stardom and predictably her marriage did not survive.

The studio moguls loved her. She had an hourglass figure and an undulating walk that made her derrière look like "two puppies fighting under a sheet," according to a Hollywood columnist; she had a half-open mouth and a whispery, breathy voice; and it seemed she was prepared to offer sexual services to just about anyone who asked. Bigger movie parts followed, her name was changed to Marilyn Monroe, and at last her breakthrough came when director John Huston cast her as a criminal's mistress in *The Asphalt Jungle* (1950). She was good, and won another mistress role in *All About Eve* the same year. But inside she was cracking up in the midst of all those sharks trying to get a piece of her, talking about her as though she were a piece of meat, and pawing her ample breasts in public. When she met Arthur Miller in 1951, first on the Fox lot and then at a party a few days later, she expected him to be the same as the rest of them. Instead he talked to her about theater and suggested she head to New York to train as an actress and develop her talent. They chatted until the early hours of the morning and he didn't even try to get her into bed afterward. "It was like running into a tree," she said later, "You know, like a cool drink when you've got a fever." It was a meeting that would change the entire course of both their lives—for better and for worse.

AN EMERGING TALENT

Arthur's father was a Polish immigrant, a tall silent man who ran a successful coat- and suit-making company in New York City. The business collapsed after the stock-market crash of 1929 and his glamorous mother was forced to sell her fur coats and jewels, for which she bitterly berated her husband. Arthur was admitted to the University of Ann Arbor in Michigan, where he studied journalism then switched

BELOW
The director Elia Kazan described Marilyn as "a decent-hearted kid whom Hollywood had brought down, legs apart. She had a thin skin and a soul that hungered for acceptance."

to English after a play he wrote, called *No Villain*, won
an award. It was at university he met his first wife, a
serious, intellectual girl named Mary Grace Slattery.
She dropped out of university to follow him to New
York after he graduated, and they lived together for
two years before getting married in August 1940. Mary
firmly believed in Arthur's talent and worked as a
waitress and then a magazine editor to support him while
he struggled to establish himself as a writer; it must have
been a tough life after their children were born, a girl in 1944
and a boy three years later. Fortunately, in 1947, the year his
second child was born, Arthur had his first hit with a play called
All My Sons, a wartime story about an airplane manufacturer
who cuts corners with tragic consequences. It won the Drama
Critics' Circle Award for the best new play of the season,
establishing him as a name on Broadway. *Death of a
Salesman*, about the unstable, down-on-his-luck Willie
Loman and his family, proved he was no one-hit wonder,
winning him the prestigious Pulitzer Prize in 1951 and
making him a rich man. But by this time his marriage was
failing. Mary was supportive but humorless and any spark
had gone. "For a man of 35, I seemed to have done nothing
but work," he said later. "When, I wondered, does one
cease to work and start to live."

He traveled to Los Angeles in 1951 with director Elia Kazan,
hoping to raise finances for a screenplay he had written entitled
The Hook. They watched Marilyn at work on the set of a movie
called *As Young as You Feel*, and then they were introduced:
"When we shook hands, the shock of her body's motion sped
through me," Arthur recalled. At the party a few days later, he
overheard someone commenting that the men present would "eat
[Marilyn] alive" and it made him feel protective so he sat down to talk
to her. She seemed gentle and sensitive, with a warm sense of humor,
and not at all the dizzy blonde she tended to portray on screen. She
was moved by his respectful attitude; no one had taken her acting
seriously before, never mind asking her opinions, and it inspired
her to improve herself. After their meeting she signed up to study
literature and art at the University of California and Arthur sent her
a reading list. They wouldn't see each other again for four years, in
which time she would have married and divorced another husband,

but they never stopped thinking about one another. She told friends, "I used to think he might see me in a movie and I wanted to do my best because he had said he thought I ought to act on stage." Arthur often bicycled or drove around Brooklyn in the evening and thought about Marilyn all the way out in California. He said later that there were times "when I was on the verge of turning my steering wheel west and jamming the pedal to the floor."

"THE EGGHEAD & THE HOURGLASS"

In January 1954, after they had been dating for two years, Marilyn married baseball star Joe DiMaggio, an all-American hero of Italian descent. He was a good man who wanted to look after her but he soon grew to resent the movie business. He hated the fact that his wife was continually cast as a slut and he had to watch her kissing other men on screen, so he urged her to give up work. He'd retired from baseball when they married and wanted a quiet home life, spending time with family and friends. She tried to mold herself into the housewife role but soon got bored and their marriage foundered just nine months after the wedding.

BELOW
Joe DiMaggio was a hugely successful baseball hero, best-known for his extraordinary 56-game hitting streak in 1941. Marilyn wasn't impressed, complaining, "He's so boring I could scream. All he knows and talks about is baseball."

In December 1954 Marilyn decided to head east, to New York, to study acting just as Arthur had suggested. She signed up for classes at the Actors Studio, run by Paula Strasberg, who would become an influential friend and mentor, and she contacted Arthur to let him know she was in town. He rushed round to see her and throughout 1955 they met frequently, often going bicycling together or spending time at her plush apartment in the Waldorf Astoria. Inevitably, they became lovers, and this period was idyllically happy, as they talked and made love and talked some more. Marilyn loved his intellect and yearned to educate herself to keep up with him in conversation. He was enthralled by her combination of sexiness and innocence, calling her "the most womanly woman I can imagine . . . She's a kind of lodestone that draws out of the male animal his essential qualities." He had been shy at college and

had never experienced this kind of passion with Mary, so the affair was a revelation. In October 1955, when his wife found out about it, she was incandescent with rage. She threw him out of the house and refused to take him back again even when he begged her. In March 1956, Arthur bowed to her wishes and went to Nevada to get a divorce. The terms were very much in Mary's favor—she got custody of both children, ownership of their Brooklyn house, generous child support, and a percentage of his earnings for life. But he was a free man.

Arthur had other problems on his mind in 1956, having been subpoenaed by the House Committee on Un-American Activities, which was engaged in rooting out figures in the media who had communist tendencies and might try to influence the American public. During his hearing, Arthur was asked the reason for a forthcoming trip to England, and he sprang a surprise on court reporters—and on Marilyn—when he said that he would be traveling to see a production of his play *A View From the Bridge* along with the woman who would by then be his wife. It was the first time he had mentioned marriage to Marilyn and she was stunned and overjoyed. There was no question that she would say yes; she was completely smitten.

ABOVE
"I love being married to Arthur Miller," Marilyn said. "All my life I've been alone. Now for the first time . . . I feel I'm not alone any more."

THE HUAC

Hollywood was a particular target of the House Committee on Un-American Activities led by Senator Joe McCarthy, and several of Arthur's left-wing friends appeared as witnesses. Some, such as Elia Kazan, were "friendly witnesses" who told all they knew and named others whom they believed to have communist sympathies. Others, such as playwright Lillian Hellman and her lover, detective novelist Dashiel Hammett, pleaded the Fifth Amendment, refusing to answer any questions on the grounds that they had a right not to incriminate themselves. When he took the stand, Arthur chose a different route: he answered directly all the questions he was asked but refused to name anyone else, and his articulate responses often left the Committee members looking foolish. Arthur was found guilty of one count of contempt but did not have to serve any time in jail (unlike Hammett). He always believed that he was only summoned because of his association with Marilyn; the Committee had hoped she might be persuaded to speak out in support of them, but instead she publicly supported Arthur.

Arthur finished giving his testimony on June 21, 1956, and he and Marilyn married eight days later. The press coverage was headlined "Egghead Weds Hourglass." She stepped into the role of Mrs. Arthur Miller, charming his parents and his children, cooking, cleaning, and playing housewife for him. But the part had never suited her and it wasn't long before they were off to England for her next movie role—and Arthur saw a side of her he had not been aware of before.

CRACKING UP

Marilyn had never behaved professionally on movie sets, which she found very stressful. She turned up late, couldn't remember her lines, and asked for umpteen breaks in filming while she consulted her guru Paula Strasberg about the best way to play a scene, clashing with any directors who disagreed. Arthur got a taste of this behavior while she was filming The Prince and the Showgirl (1957) with Laurence Olivier, and he also realized she was trying to mask her insecurities by swallowing pills by the handful and washing them down with alcohol. He wrote in his diary, "She was like a smashed vase. It is a beautiful thing when it is intact, but the broken pieces are murderous and they can cut you." He left his diary lying out and she read the entry, devastated to learn that he was already disappointed in her.

Back in New York she was bored, complaining that Arthur spent hours on end in his study with the door closed. He knew she was needy and egotistical, like a spoiled child, but he still hoped he could mend her with his love and devotion. Sadly, it soon became clear that no matter how much attention he gave her, she would always crave more. She became pregnant twice during their marriage but miscarried once, then suffered an ectopic pregnancy. She also took an overdose on at least two occasions and he had to rush her to hospital to have her stomach pumped. He had underestimated the extent of her mental-health problems and overestimated his ability to deal with them.

It must have been humiliating for Arthur when Marilyn had a very public affair with French actor Yves Montand while filming *Let's Make*

OPPOSITE
Arthur at the HUAC in June 1956. His 1953 play The Crucible, about the Salem witch trials of 1692, was an obvious satire on the Committee.

BELOW
Arthur wrote of Marilyn, "To have survived, she would have had to be either more cynical or even further from reality than she was. Instead, she was a poet on a street corner trying to recite to a crowd pulling at her clothes."

> " She was like a smashed vase. It is a beautiful thing when it is intact, but the broken pieces can cut you "

Love (1960). She knew her marriage was failing and was desperately seeking another man to take Arthur's place, but Yves was already married and had no intention of leaving his wife. Meanwhile, Arthur wrote a script called The Misfits with a role for Marilyn that he hoped would establish her as a serious dramatic actress. The shoot in the Nevada desert was troubled, though, with Marilyn bitterly berating and humiliating Arthur in public. By the end of it they were no longer on speaking terms and she was more fragile than ever. "What's very sad," he explained, "is that I had written it to make Marilyn feel good. And for her, it resulted in complete collapse." The marriage ended when filming was over. Arthur had done his best to save her but it wasn't enough and he decided he needed to save himself. She was angry, saying that Arthur had tried to fit her into an idealized image and couldn't deal with the reality of her true nature. She'd looked to him for protection and instead he patronized her and acted as though he were morally superior. "He's a cold fish," she said. "Arthur's got no sense of humor."

Although devastated by the breakup, within months Arthur had fallen in love with photographer Inge Morath, who would become his third wife in February 1962. Marilyn had affairs with Frank Sinatra, President John F. Kennedy, and then his brother Robert Kennedy, and once again found herself being treated like a piece of meat being passed from man to man. She was fired from the movie Something's Got to Give for unauthorized absences from the set, and she feared she was aging and that it would be harder to find work in the future. She was upset when she heard in spring 1962 that Arthur's new wife was pregnant, while she had never been able to have a child herself, and she feared ending up in a mental asylum as her mother had as her mental turmoil became unmanageable. Late in the evening of August 4, 1962, Marilyn's maid found her lying dead in her bed. The autopsy report said that she had taken a fatal overdose of barbiturates (prescribed sedatives). A letter she left behind suggested she might have been hoping to remarry DiMaggio, with whom she had always stayed in touch.

ABOVE
Marilyn with (from left to right) Montgomery Clift, Arthur, John Huston, and Clark Gable in publicity stills for The Misfits (1961).

OPPOSITE
In Something's Got to Give (1962). After Marilyn died, the movie was remade with a new cast and titled Move Over, Darling.

Arthur reacted coldly to the news of her death, saying to the studio publicist who informed him, "It's your problem, not mine." He did not attend the funeral, which was organized by Joe DiMaggio, and later wrote in his autobiography that it was twenty years before he could cry about it. Several of the plays he wrote later in life feature damaged characters with similarities to Marilyn, as if he was trying to work out in writing the terrible truths of their relationship. Is there anything more he could have done to save her from herself? Why did he get involved with someone who was quite so badly damaged? Had the catastrophic crash of their marriage hastened her demise? These are questions that no one now will ever be able to answer.

MARILYN'S DEATH

Friends who saw Marilyn in her final days reported her to be optimistic about the future: she was going back to work on *Something's Got to Give* and she was hoping to rekindle her relationship with Joe DiMaggio. She spoke to several people on the telephone during her last evening, and they said she sounded befuddled, as though she had taken pills, but no one was alarmed enough to check on her. Her death was not reported till the following morning, and her maid lied to police about the time she found her. Theories sprang up that she had been killed by friends of the Kennedys because she was threatening to reveal the truth about her affairs with them, which could have brought down the Presidency. Others claimed she was killed by the Mafia as revenge for Robert Kennedy's relentless pursuit of them as Attorney General. Yet more think a barbiturate enema was administered by one of her doctors, who didn't realize a separate doctor had prescribed her a different pill, creating a fatal combination. But the most likely answer is that a lonely, disturbed, 36-year-old woman swallowed handful after handful of pills in an attempt to put an end to the misery that had plagued her since birth.

RICHARD
BURTON
&
ELIZABETH
TAYLOR

RICHARD WALTER JENKINS

BORN: NOVEMBER 10, 1925
PONTRHYDYFEN, WALES

DIED: AUGUST 5, 1984
CÉLIGNY, SWITZERLAND

ELIZABETH ROSEMOND TAYLOR

BORN: FEBRUARY 27, 1932
LONDON, ENGLAND

DIED: MARCH 23, 2011
LOS ANGELES, CALIFORNIA

★

MARRIED: MARCH 15, 1964, MONTREAL, CANADA AND
OCTOBER 10, 1975, CHOBE NATIONAL PARK, BOTSWANA

RIGHT
Falling in love in Cleopatra then falling out in
Who's Afraid of Virginia Woolf? *(inset above)*

" *I will not become another notch on his belt* "

ABOVE
Elizabeth and Eddie Fisher in Paris in 1959. During the making of Cleopatra, Richard referred to Eddie as "the Waiter" because his main role seemed to be fetching Elizabeth's drinks.

RIGHT
Richard and Sybil in 1951. They always called each other "Boot," short for "beautiful" as pronounced in a Welsh accent.

The beginning of the Taylor–Burton affair was cataclysmic, like two fiery comets colliding. Marriages were destroyed, families shattered, the press were hostile, and even the Vatican cardinals felt compelled to criticize. Afterward, the beleaguered couple always referred to the furor as "Le Scandale."

When Elizabeth Taylor first met Richard Burton at a Hollywood party in 1953, she was an established star and he was the new boy in town. "He was rather full of himself," she recalled later, and she gave him what she described as "the cold fish eye." Fast-forward eight years to the summer of 1961, when she heard that Richard had been cast in the role of Marc Antony in the epic movie *Cleopatra*, in which she was playing the title role. By this time, she was the highest-paid actress on the planet, having secured an unprecedented million-dollar contract for *Cleopatra*, while he was still best known as a stage actor and a lothario, famous for seducing all his leading ladies. "I will not become another notch on his belt," Elizabeth firmly declared. But when they played their first scene together in January 1962, he was so hungover his hand shook as he tried to drink a cup of coffee and she stepped in to assist. She was touched by his fragile state and dazzled by his erudition, and before long they were sneaking off for secret trysts in their dressing rooms or in her secretary's Rome apartment.

The problem was that both were married to other people. Richard had married Welsh actress Sybil Williams back in 1949 after they met on the set of his first-ever film, *The Last Days of Dolwyn*. They had two daughters together, the youngest of whom suffered from autism. Sybil knew Richard was frequently unfaithful but turned a blind eye, confident that he would always return to her when the filming or the stage production was over. Elizabeth, meanwhile, was on her fourth marriage at the age of twenty-nine. There had been a brief first marriage to Nicky Hilton, the

BELOW
On the set of Cleopatra, 1962. At the time by far the most expensive movie ever made, it almost bankrupted Twentieth Century Fox.

hotel chain heir, which lasted only nine months due to his drinking and abusive behavior. Next came English actor Michael Wilding, twenty years older than Elizabeth, with whom she had two sons, but he was too gentle for the feisty young woman who later admitted to henpecking him. Her third husband, impresario Mike Todd, was a larger-than-life character who introduced Elizabeth to her lifelong passion for jewelry and with whom she had a daughter, but who died in a plane crash thirteen months after their marriage. In deepest mourning, Elizabeth turned for comfort to Todd's best friend, Eddie Fisher, a popular crooner who was married at the time to the squeaky-clean actress Debbie Reynolds. The inevitable happened, they fell in love, and Elizabeth's name was blackened in the moralistic 1959 press coverage, which of course made her headline news. Arriving in Rome to film *Cleopatra* in September 1961, she had only just regained a little public sympathy after a severe bout of pneumonia the previous March, in which her life was saved by an emergency tracheotomy.

It seemed Richard had nothing to lose if their affair was revealed; in fact, being associated with the most famous woman on the planet would most likely help his career. But Elizabeth was streetwise enough to recognize she would be crucified by the media. No matter how unfairly, she would get the blame for breaking up his marriage and her own. And yet she simply couldn't help herself.

BELOW
"I've always admitted that I'm ruled by my passions," Elizabeth said. "I have a woman's body and a child's emotions."

A CRAVING FOR LOVE

Both Richard and Elizabeth had troubled childhoods, but for quite different reasons. Richard's mother died in childbirth before his second birthday, leaving him with eleven older siblings and a father addicted to alcohol and gambling. His sister Cecilia and her husband took in the young boy, and his brother Ifor was a strong influence, but his father was largely absent from his early life in the Welsh village of Pontrhydyfen. Richard excelled at sports, especially rugby, but he also loved literature and drama. An inspiring schoolteacher, Philip H. Burton, took the boy under his wing, teaching him to lose his Welsh accent and giving him exercises to develop his distinctive voice. Richard left school at the age of sixteen to earn money, but Burton persuaded him to continue his studies and, when he began to get acting parts, Richard adopted his teacher's surname as his stage name.

During World War II, Richard served as a navigator in the Royal Air Force. In 1947 he moved to London, signed up with a theatrical agency and began working in British movies and theater productions. After his 1951 Prince Hal in *Henry IV, Part I,* renowned theater critic Kenneth Tynan wrote: "In the first intermission, local critics stood agape in the lobby." He was admitted to the postwar theatrical in-crowd, a group that included John Gielgud, Paul Scofield, and Michael Redgrave, and achieved acclaim in virtually every role. In 1952, he made his first Hollywood movie, starring opposite Olivia de Havilland in *My Cousin Rachel,* and earned his first Golden Globe.

ABOVE
A young Richard. "I rather like my reputation—that of a spoiled genius from the Welsh gutter, a drunk, a womanizer; it's rather an attractive image."

Sybil, by then his wife, put her own acting career on the back burner to travel around with him as he juggled both stage and screen roles. She must have been hurt by his affairs with costars (including Claire Bloom, Angie Dickinson, Lee Remick, Lana Turner, and Jean Simmons) but Sybil was the warm-hearted, sensible Welsh girl who looked after him and gave him stability in an otherwise rootless existence. Only one thing threatened his rise and it came in a bottle. Richard appeared to have his father's gene for alcoholism and his capacity for drinking, even in his teens and twenties, was legendary. He later said he turned to the bottle "to burn up the flatness, the stale, empty, dull deadness that one feels when one goes offstage." Perhaps that also explains the promiscuity. No matter how many ecstatic reviews he received, he seemed to need something else to make him feel whole.

Elizabeth Taylor was a Hollywood child star who chafed under the pressure of a stereotypical pushy mother. She was born in North London but her family was American and in 1939 they sailed home for the duration of the war. Elizabeth was cast in her first movie, *There's One Born Every Minute,* at the age of nine, after her mother heard the studios were looking for pretty young girls and took her for a screen test. Elizabeth was extraordinarily beautiful even as a child, with dark

> **"I was taught by my parents that if you fall in love . . . you get married"**

ABOVE
National Velvet, 1944.
"Some of my best
leading men have
been dogs and horses,"
Elizabeth quipped.

OPPOSITE
Elizabeth and Richard
on a yacht off the island
of Ischia, June 1962, as
filming on Cleopatra
drew to a close.

blue eyes that up close gave the impression of being violet, and a double row of eyelashes. She first achieved fame working with a dog in *Lassie Come Home* (1943), then a horse in *National Velvet* (1944), and MGM tied her to a contract which, according to her, made her an "MGM chattel" for the next eighteen years. At sixteen she announced she wanted to quit acting, but her mother wouldn't allow it, telling her she had a responsibility to her family and to her public. It was partly to get away from parental pressure that Elizabeth leaped into her doomed first marriage, and thereafter she kept on marrying every man she fell in love with. "I was taught by my parents that if you fall in love . . . you get married. I guess I'm very old-fashioned," she later explained.

In other ways, Elizabeth was an exceptionally modern woman for her day. By the time she accepted the part in *Cleopatra*, she was negotiating her own contracts with the studios and setting her own terms. Her best friends were gay men in an era when homosexuality was still illegal. And she took her children with her to foreign cities and movie sets, eager to bring them up with a warmth she felt had been lacking in her own upbringing. She enjoyed a cocktail or two but she wasn't a hard drinker until she met Richard Burton. She was frequently ill, with a bad back, painful periods, and a weak chest, and she took pills to combat her various ailments. But her chief problem when she started work on *Cleopatra* was that she had fallen out of love with Eddie Fisher and there was a vacancy in her life for a lover who could both stand up to her and keep her enthralled. More than anything else, Elizabeth liked to be in love.

LE SCANDALE

The affair became common knowledge on the *Cleopatra* set after Richard and Elizabeth, in their Antony and Cleopatra costumes, carried on kissing during a scene while the director repeatedly called "Cut!" Soon the paparazzi were buzzing around trying to get the picture that would prove the rumors. Twentieth Century Fox publicists denied the story, but within weeks a photographer snapped a long-lens shot of

Elizabeth and Richard kissing outside her dressing room. Sybil put her foot down, Richard ended the affair, Elizabeth took a few pills too many in what appears to have been a dramatic gesture rather than a genuine suicide attempt—and before long they were back together again. Over Easter 1962, they sneaked off to the Italian island of Santo Stefano, hoping for some private time, but instead the world's media arrived and besieged them in their villa. It was after that fiasco that a group of Vatican cardinals wrote an article about Ms. Taylor, accusing her of "erotic vagrancy" and berating her for setting a bad example for her children. "These children need an honored name more than a famous name, a serious mother more than a beautiful mother," they wrote. It must have been distressing, but Elizabeth wouldn't give up the relationship. "Richard and I had an incredible chemistry together," she explained later in life. "We couldn't get enough of each other."

Richard was under pressure from his wife and his brother Ifor to end the affair. Ifor was incensed on Sybil's behalf and traveled over to Rome to remonstrate with Richard, even punching him during an argument. His British theatrical friends warned him not to get drawn into Elizabeth's stellar orbit. Laurence Olivier cabled him: "Make up your mind, dear heart. Do you want to be a great actor or a household word?" Richard's reply was, "Both." Elizabeth's marriage to Eddie Fisher ended after he

PAPARAZZI

The term "paparazzi" came from the name of a photojournalist character in Fellini's 1960 film *La Dolce Vita*. He told *Time* magazine that the name suggested "a buzzing insect, hovering, darting, stinging." In Rome in the early 60s, paparazzi rode around on Vespas taking shots of the international celebrities who frequented cafés and restaurants around the Via Veneto. Their methods of getting a good shot could include shouting insults at the subject, attempting to trip them up, and even throwing drinks. Elizabeth and Richard were hounded by paparazzi from the moment they arrived in Rome. Photographers climbed the trees surrounding her villa to photograph her children in the swimming pool and on one occasion they forced her car off the road. Richard had to repress his famous Welsh temper and restrain himself from striking out at them on many an occasion. Paparazzi tried to bribe *Cleopatra* employees to sneak photographs on set: one girl was found with a miniature camera hidden in her beehive hairstyle.

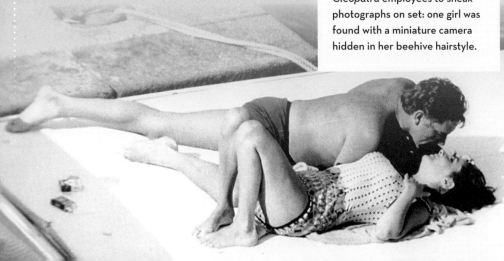

skulked back to New York to cry on the shoulder of anyone who would listen, but still Richard wouldn't give up his marriage, his rock. Filming ended, he had one "final" holiday with Elizabeth, then rejoined Sybil and his daughters at their villa in Switzerland. But Elizabeth decamped to her own Swiss villa just a short drive across the mountains, from where she kept calling him. She wasn't going to let go so easily. For her, it wasn't just about sexual chemistry. Richard was the first lover who told her she was intelligent and asked her opinion on literature and acting; she'd had a disrupted education, basically being tutored between takes on movies, and this was the compliment that meant the most to her.

There was some going back and forth, but by the time *Cleopatra* premiered in June 1963, Sybil had agreed to divorce Richard, and in March 1964 he married Elizabeth in Montreal, where he was appearing on stage. Her magnetism had simply been too great. He wrote of her in his 1968 diary, "She is a wildly exciting lover-mistress, she is shy and witty, she is nobody's fool. She is a brilliant actress, she is beautiful beyond the dreams of pornography . . . And I shall love her forever."

DIAMONDS, COCKTAILS, & PRETTY GIRLS

Everything about the Burton-Taylor marriage was excessive: the diamonds he bought her, their yacht *Kalizma*, the houses, the parties, and the sheer quantity of alcohol consumed. Still they managed to do some good acting work, in particular the 1966 movie *Who's Afraid of Virginia Woolf?* in which they played a drunken couple arguing themselves to destruction. The portrayal of a disintegrating marriage was rather close to the bone, and both would say later that it took its toll on their own relationship. The alcohol caused damage, as did her health problems—she had to have a hysterectomy in the late 60s and her back pain went from bad to worse. But on paper it was Richard's infidelities that brought about the end of the marriage. Elizabeth had told him early on that she would not tolerate him being unfaithful and for a long time he wasn't, but in 1969 during the filming of *Anne of the Thousand Days*, he had an affair with his costar Geneviève Bujold while Elizabeth was in the hospital. In 1972, he romanced Nathalie Delon during the filming of *Bluebeard*, and the final straw came in 1974 when he flew to California without Elizabeth to make a movie called *The Klansman.* Soon he was reported to be carousing with a teenage waitress called Pepsi, as well as an unnamed hotel receptionist. Elizabeth decided enough was enough and, heartbroken, she filed for divorce.

> "*She is beautiful beyond the dreams of pornography . . . And I shall love her forever*"

They went their separate ways but didn't get over each other, and when they met in the summer of 1975 to discuss financial matters, they ended up crying in each other's arms. They wed again, in Botswana, but the marriage was short-lived and ended after Richard took up with Suzy Hunt, a model who would soon become his third wife. Elizabeth married a Republican senator, John Warner, but became depressed and admitted herself to the Betty Ford Center to deal with her addiction to painkillers.

In 1983, Elizabeth made one final attempt to reunite with Richard by persuading him to appear with her

BELOW
On the set of The V.I.P.s *(1963), the second movie they made together. It did well at the box office because of the huge public interest in the star couple.*

ELIZABETH TAYLOR'S JEWELRY

Elizabeth developed a love of expensive jewelry during her twenties, and Richard soon realized that he was expected to contribute to her collection. He bought her some exquisite pieces from the Bulgari store in Rome during the filming of *Cleopatra*, but his most extravagant purchases came after their marriage. The Krupp diamond is a huge 33.19-carat diamond he purchased for her in 1968, which she set in a ring and wore every day. The pear-shaped Taylor-Burton diamond, which he bought her the following year, was even bigger at 69.2 carats and was the first diamond ever to sell for more than a million dollars. The 50-carat La Peregrina pearl dates back to the 16th century and had been owned by Mary I of England, Margaret of Austria, and Napoleon's brother Joseph Bonaparte, among others, before Richard bought it in 1969. In 1970, he gave her the so-called "Ping-pong Diamonds" after she beat him at a game of table tennis. When the extraordinary collection was auctioned on behalf of her beloved AIDS charities after her death, it raised more than $115 million.

in a production of *Private Lives* on Broadway. He was dating a production assistant called Sally Hay and was off the booze, but Elizabeth was still drinking. The play was a laughingstock, partly because she was frequently drunk on stage, and during the run Richard slipped off to marry Sally in Las Vegas. He was fifty-seven and his health was badly damaged by the decades of alcohol abuse. The following year he died of a brain hemorrhage while at his house in Switzerland. Elizabeth is said to have fainted when she heard the news.

She took one more husband after Richard's death, a construction worker called Larry Fortensky, but the marriage didn't last and she admitted, "Richard is the only one I truly loved and still care about. I shall miss him till the day I die." She claimed that the week before his death he had written her a final love letter, which she took with her to her own grave in 2011.

In some ways their story is a tragedy of two alcoholics who had a passionate, explosive relationship while drunk and who never managed to get sober at the same time. Many believe that Richard did not fulfill his huge potential as an actor because of his decadent lifestyle with Elizabeth. But there's no question that they loved each other obsessively, with every fiber of their beings, in the years they were together. "Maybe we loved each other too much," Elizabeth mused toward the end of her life. She was sure that if Richard had lived, they would have married again.

> " *Richard is the only one I truly loved and still care about. I shall miss him till the day I die* "

RIGHT
Richard said of their relationship, "You can't keep clapping a couple of sticks of dynamite together without expecting them to blow up."

LEFT
"Big girls need big diamonds," according to Elizabeth. Here she is wearing the 33-karat Krupp diamond which Richard bought for her in 1968 for $305,000.

STEVE MCQUEEN & ALI MACGRAW

TERENCE STEVEN MCQUEEN

BORN: MARCH 24, 1930
BEECH GROVE, INDIANA

DIED: NOVEMBER 7, 1980
CIUDAD JUÁREZ, MEXICO

ELIZABETH ALICE MACGRAW

BORN: APRIL 1, 1939
POUND RIDGE, NEW YORK

★

MARRIED: AUGUST 31, 1973
CHEYENNE, WYOMING

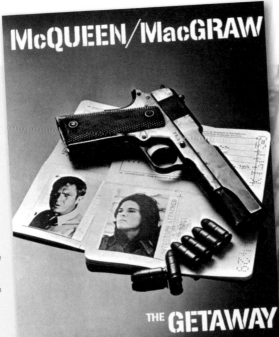

McQUEEN/MacGRAW

THE GETAWAY

OPPOSITE
Ali and Steve during the filming of The Getaway *(1972). Her husband Bob was in New York making* The Godfather.

LEFT
"I believe in me," Steve
said. "I'm a little screwed
up but I'm beautiful." By
contrast, Ali was under-
confident both about
her looks and her acting.

When Ali was offered a part in the movie *The Getaway*, she didn't want to do it. Not because it was a bad script or a difficult role, but because as soon as she laid eyes on the leading man, Steve McQueen, she knew without a shadow of a doubt that she would get into trouble with him.

————————

*B*oth Steve and Ali were damaged by dysfunctional childhoods: the children of alcoholics, they had been beaten by their parents or guardians when young. They embarked on their relationship still suffering the effects of those childhood wounds and trying to find salvation in each other. It was not an ideal beginning—but at the same time, there's no question that they were madly, devotedly, completely, and utterly in love.

It's hardly surprising that Steve found it impossible to trust women, having become used to his mother abandoning him whenever a new man came into her life. His father had walked out when he was six months old, and between the ages of three and eight—formative years—Steve was brought up by his Uncle Claude, a god-fearing Missouri farmer. Young Steve learned to work hard—he got a thrashing when he didn't—and he also learned to use his fists against the kids who taunted him for being fatherless. Throughout this time, he didn't receive any letters or birthday cards from his mother and only saw her once, but when he was eight she decided he should come and live with her and her new husband. His stepfather sided against him from the start and there were violent confrontations. "He worked me over pretty good," Steve remembered, "and my mother didn't lift a hand."

He turned to street gangs and fell into petty crime, enjoying the element of danger. Unable to cope, his mother sent him back to Uncle Claude, but when Steve was twelve she summoned him to live with her and yet another new husband. This time, after he was caught stealing hubcaps, she signed him in to reform school, an act for which he never forgave her. He spent fourteen months at the Junior Boys Republic in Chino, California, where he found himself frequently punished for bucking the system. When he reached sixteen, his mother insisted he leave the school and come to New York, where she now had yet another new lover, but when he arrived it transpired she had changed her mind and didn't want him there in case it jeopardized her budding romance. Steve had had enough. He met a couple of sailors and got

With his piercing blue eyes and sandy-blond hair, girls flocked to him

work on their ship sailing to the Dominican Republic, then at the age of seventeen he applied for the Marine Corps and spent three years training with them. If it hadn't been for that, he freely admitted, "I would have ended up in jail or something. I was a wild child."

Along the way, there had already been dozens of women. Among many odd jobs Steve had taken, there had been work as a towel-bearer in brothels, and one of the perks was being allowed to sample the goods. It wasn't just prostitutes he slept with, though—with his piercing blue eyes and sandy-blond hair, girls tended to flock to him. Back in New York, one girlfriend suggested he tried acting classes, and that led to TV parts, and then, in 1956, his first movie success as a knife-wielding punk in *Somebody Up There Likes Me*. He began to earn money in motorcycle racing, too, becoming very successful and buying himself a Harley Davidson, the first of many bikes he would own. In 1956 he married Neile Adams, a petite, beautiful dancer of Filipino heritage who was earning plenty of money and was happy to support him.

BELOW
Steve was a loving husband to Neile but on the side he boasted of getting "more pussy than Frank Sinatra."

Although she was the main wage earner, he still expected her to be the perfect wife and when she served up a quick dinner made from frozen food one night before rushing out to perform in a show, he threw it across the room in disgust. He wanted it all— a wife who brought in the money, was a domestic goddess, and was completely faithful to him, in spite of the promiscuous habits he retained from the days before they were married. According to a friend, Steve was "virtually a sex machine." He liked his women singly or in pairs and couldn't let a day go by without having sex. When asked why he chose acting as a career, he once explained, frankly, that it was because "There were more chicks in the acting profession who did it."

MEETING THE PERFECT GIRL

Ali's childhood wasn't quite as awful as Steve's. On paper, it looked idyllic: growing up in a small New England town, with dreams of being a ballet dancer or an intellectual on Paris's Left Bank. She thrived at school and enjoyed appearing in school plays, having a rich imaginative life, as well as spending plenty of time exploring the outdoors with her younger brother. But the dark shadow over them both was her father's unpredictable personality and frequent violence. He was a bitter man with a drinking habit who took out his frustrations on his children. Ali attempted to curb his violence by being a good daughter: "I put all my energy into trying to correct the chaos in our life. I was the Perfect Girl—capital P, capital G." As a result, her brother bore the brunt of the attacks while she was unable to protect him. On leaving school she won a scholarship to the prestigious Wellesley College, Massachusetts, and while there met the man who would be her first husband. Robin Hoen was a great catch—the supersmart son of a prominent neurosurgeon—but she soon got bored. Life was too exciting in the early 1960s to be tied down to any one man and after a year they divorced.

In 1960, Ali had begun working for Diana Vreeland, fashion editor at *Harper's Bazaar*, and developed her own unique sense of style, which borrowed from the hippie clothes of the era. She became a photographer's assistant and was asked to model for a Chanel advert, for which she had to pose naked under a Puerto Rican waterfall. The resulting image appeared on posters across America and led to a movie agent tracking her down and taking her on. She was soon cast in the romantic comedy *Goodbye, Columbus* (1969), in which she plays a wealthy college student who falls for a working-class boy. As a result of this, she was offered a role in a movie called *Love Story*, the only catch being that it hadn't yet been signed by a studio. She went to visit top producer Bob Evans, promptly got drunk, and fell into his swimming pool. Fortunately,

BELOW
Ali always had a distinctive and much-imitated sense of style, but believed she was "not pale enough, too bold in the eyebrow department" ever to make it as a top model.

THE MAGNIFICENT SEVEN

In March 1960, producer/director John Sturges brought together a cast of relative unknowns to make a movie about seven American gunmen hired to protect a Mexican village from bandits. Yul Brynner (as one of the gunmen) and Eli Wallach (head of the bandits) were already names, but Steve McQueen, Charles Bronson, James Coburn, Robert Vaughn, Brad Dexter, and Horst Buchholz were still trying to establish themselves, and that led to fierce competition for the limelight during the filming. In an early scene, as the seven cross a river on their way to the Mexican village, Steve McQueen casually leans down from his horse to scoop up some water in his hat, an unscripted moment that typifies his scene-stealing antics throughout the filming. Yul Brynner was concerned that he should look taller than McQueen and stood on a little mound of earth for their scenes together, but as soon as he got a chance Steve kicked it away. He also fingers his hat and employs other little tricks to distract attention during Yul's dialogue, which led to tension between the two but was highly amusing for the older hands on set.

RIGHT
The Magnificent Seven ride into town.

he was smitten with her and agreed to make the movie. He also persuaded her to move in and marry him, and so she found herself living in the lap of luxury in his Beverly Hills mansion, surrounded by servants. When *Love Story* came out in 1970, it was a huge hit, bringing her overnight fame for her portrayal of the snappy-talking college girl who falls in love then succumbs to cancer. She and Bob had a son, Josh, in 1971 and for a while life was rosy.

Steve McQueen saw Ali in *Love Story* and requested she play the part of his wife in *The Getaway* (1972). By this time Steve was one of the most bankable stars in Hollywood, with portrayals of tough loners in such films as *The Magnificent Seven* (1960), *The Great Escape* (1963), and *Bullitt* (1968). He was touchy and difficult to work with but his macho, antihero image and his cool, don't-give-a-damn attitude made women flock to the movie theaters to see him. He came to Bob and Ali's mansion for a meeting about *The Getaway* and, as Ali wrote in her autobiography, "I remember sitting in the projection room and seeing Steve on the other side of the swimming pool, and you could see those eyes—the most extraordinary blue." She was gorgeous herself, with big dark eyes and long curtains of dark hair, and Steve lusted after her from the first

moment he saw her. His marriage to Neile had ended a few months earlier after he pulled a gun on her and forced her to confess to a one-night stand with another actor, reportedly beating her up afterward. His mistrust of women had increased over the years, and it often triggered rages, some of which became violent. Neile wasn't putting up with it. She divorced him and by the time he flew to Texas to begin filming *The Getaway*, he was a single man.

Steve and Ali's affair began almost immediately. "I was obsessed with Steve from the moment he stepped into my world," Ali later said, "and there was never enough air for me to breathe to change that feeling." Steve was hooked as well. "This is the first time in my life that I have no desire or even thought of sleeping around," he told a friend. "This is the person I want to be with for the rest of my life."

ABOVE
Ali with then-husband Bob Evans and on the set of The Getaway *with Steve (below).*

RIGHT
A scene in The Getaway. *According to Ali, "There was that electric feeling you have when you are first in love—a kind of omnipotence and even madness that anyone within a fifty-foot range can feel."*

LIVING ON THE BEACH

Filming on *The Getaway* took three months, and Steve and Ali's passionate romance was the talk of the set. However, contrary to what he had told his friend, Steve didn't manage to be faithful, and made no attempt to hide his infidelities from her during this time, openly chatting up the groupies who pursued him wherever he went and often taking girls back to his trailer. At the same time he interrogated Ali if she so much as glanced at another man. He called her "Old Lady" and ordered her to cook his breakfast, get him a beer, and generally do his bidding. During her time in New York, Ali had briefly shared an apartment with feminist trailblazer Gloria Steinem but she forsook any modern ideas about equality in relationships to mold herself into the woman Steve wanted her to be. She knew she wasn't his physical type—he preferred blondes for his flings—and she strove to make herself more desirable to him, the man she considered the most desirable on the planet.

After filming finished, Ali briefly returned to Bob but the magnetic pull she felt for Steve was simply too strong. She had to be with him. They rented neighboring houses in LA's Coldwater Canyon then, after he finished filming *Papillon* (1973), in which he played a prisoner in a brutal prison who has been falsely accused of murder, they moved into a beach house in the small town of Trancas near Malibu. Her son, Josh, and his son, Chad, joined them, although his daughter chose to stay with her mother. Steve insisted from the start that Ali give up work to keep house for him, and she complied. They spent their days surfing in the ocean or riding through the desert on one of Steve's precious motorcycles, and there were many wonderful times. "Being with him was like a drug high," she said later. "It was either great days or horrendous days, and nothing in between." They enjoyed having neighbors over for potluck suppers and leading a normal, noncelebrity lifestyle. One night, after a huge fight, Steve casually proposed, saying, "Okay, baby. If you want to get married, it's tomorrow or never." With just their children in tow, they drove to Cheyenne, Wyoming, far from the Hollywood press pack, and tied the knot in front of a rather startled justice of the peace who had been summoned from a round of golf. Immediately afterward, Steve insisted that Ali sign a prenup, claiming that Neile had taken him to the cleaners after their divorce and he didn't want to risk the same happening again. She was distressed at the negative omen but complied for the sake of tranquility.

It wasn't long before rumors reached Ali that Steve was keeping a suite at the Beverly Wilshire hotel in which to entertain girls for sex, but she chose to turn a blind eye. He smoked pot, drank beer or wine, and dabbled with LSD and cocaine, but she had a taste for hard liquor herself so it didn't seem like an issue. Her main problem was in trying to be someone she wasn't. In reality, she was an East Coast intellectual who liked ballet

> *"Okay, baby. If you want to get married, it's tomorrow or never."*

BELOW
Steve called Ali his "New York intellectual" and seemed to like the fact that she'd been to college and could be sophisticated when the occasion required it.

THE BETTY FORD CLINIC

In 1978 the wife of President Gerald Ford was forced by her family to accept that she was addicted to booze and painkillers. First Lady Betty Ford sought treatment and in 1982 decided to set up a clinic where other people in her position could get help. The facility at Rancho Mirage, California, provides a safe place for addicts to detox, and also helps them to address the pain in their lives that led them to seek anesthesia through alcohol or drugs. By admitting her own troubles so publicly, Betty Ford helped destigmatize addiction, and in December 1983 Elizabeth Taylor became the first major star to seek treatment at the center. Other celebrities followed, from Mary Tyler Moore and Johnny Cash to Ali MacGraw. It is no five-star hotel. Stars have to do their own laundry and cleaning just like every other resident, something Taylor resisted at first. At group therapy meetings, they are forced to reveal their demons with lacerating honesty and oversized egos are deflated. It was tough, but for Ali MacGraw, at least, it was the start of a whole new life that involved taking care of herself and led her to become a yoga devotee.

and opera and yearned to travel to Paris, rather than living the quasi-hermit lifestyle of West Coast beach bum. The strain of the pretense made her "Tight. Judgemental. Simmering," she later wrote in her autobiography.

They would get along peacefully for a while, then a fight would erupt seemingly out of nowhere, and during one such spat Steve hit her across the face, breaking the skin by her eyebrow. The incident shocked them both, and they agreed he would leave the house and stay elsewhere whenever they argued to avoid it happening again. When Ali suffered a miscarriage, the relationship deteriorated further. Realizing she would be penniless if they separated, she accepted a job in a movie called Convoy (1978), but when she told Steve he declared, "In that case we are filing for divorce." She took the job anyway, and in an attempt to make peace Steve came to join her on set. But during the drive back to Trancas, he interrogated her relentlessly about whether she had been flirting with a man over dinner and finally she'd had enough. She made him stop the car and screamed that their marriage was over—and she meant it. Steve sobbed when he told a friend about their breakup.

FIGHTING FOR LIFE

Shortly after the end of his marriage to Ali, Steve went to the doctor complaining of a persistent cough. He underwent various tests and was diagnosed as having a type of lung cancer associated with exposure to asbestos. (He had once been given the task of removing asbestos lagging from pipework on a ship while in the Marines, and this is a possible cause.) While undergoing cancer treatment, he got married for a third time—to a model named Barbara Minty—and according to her he became an Evangelical Christian in the last months of his life. When medics in the US said there was nothing more they could do to help him, he flew to Mexico to undergo a controversial treatment that involved coffee enemas and injections of live cells from cows and sheep. He was only fifty years old and desperate to live, but following surgery to remove some tumors he suffered a heart attack and died. Ali had not visited him in the Mexican clinic, but all the same she had been desperately sad to hear of his illness. Steve's first wife Neile called to tell her the news of his death and later they held a memorial service for him.

Ali's journey wasn't over. She never remarried but in the mid-1980s had a life-changing revelation when she checked herself into the Betty Ford Clinic for recovering addicts. They helped her to analyze the way her father's influence had made her dependent on the wrong kind of men, and she finally accepted that she was in fact an alcoholic. Steve had been pretty much stoned every day she knew him, so in truth their marriage never had much of a chance, but still Ali could never regret it. "It was very, very passionate, and dramatic, and hurtful, and ecstatic," she says. According to a close friend, Steve, "loved Ali MacGraw more than he loved anyone else in his entire life. Until the day he died he was madly in love with her."

> *"Steve loved Ali MacGraw more than he loved anyone else in his entire life. Until the day he died he was madly in love with her"*

BELOW
Ali describes her relationship with Steve as "pretty much a wipeout for both of us." "But," she adds, "I think it would have been impossible not to fall in love with [him]."

Douglas Fairbanks & Mary Pickford

PBS, Mary Pickford, *American Experience* interview (at http://www.pbs.org/wgbh/amex/pickford/filmmore/pt.html)

Vance, Jeffrey, *Douglas Fairbanks*, University of California Press, 2008

Whitfield, Eileen, *Pickford: The Woman Who Made Hollywood*, University Press of Kentucky, 1997

Rudolph Valentino & Natacha Rambova

Botham, Noel, *Valentino: The First Superstar*, Metro Publishing, London, 2002

Leider, Emily, *Dark Lover: The Life and Death of Rudolph Valentino*, Farrar, Straus & Giroux, New York, 2003

Stutesman, Drake, "Natacha Rambova," Columbia University Women Film Pioneers Project (at https://wfpp.cdrs.columbia.edu/pioneer/ccp-natacha-rambova)

John Gilbert & Greta Garbo

Bret, David, *Greta Garbo, A Divine Star*, Robson Press, London, 2012

Fountain, Leatrice Gilbert, *Dark Star: The Untold Story of the Meteoric Rise and Fall of the Legendary John Gilbert*, St Martin's Press, New York, 1985

Golden, Eve, *John Gilbert: The Last of the Silent Film Stars*, University Press of Kentucky, 2013

Swenson, Karen, *Greta Garbo, A Life Apart*, Simon & Schuster, London 1997

Clark Gable & Carole Lombard

Harris, Warren G., *Gable and Lombard*, Simon & Schuster, New York and London, 1974

Harris, Warren G., *Clark Gable: A Biography*, Three Rivers Press, New York, 2002

Lewis, Judy, *Uncommon Knowledge*, Pocket Books, New York, 1994

Swindell, Larry, *Screwball: The Life of Carole Lombard*, William Morrow & Co, New York, 1975

Spencer Tracy & Katharine Hepburn

Curtis, James, *Spencer Tracy, A Biography*, Knopf Publishing Group, New York and London, 2011

Hepburn, Katharine, *Me: Stories of My Life*, Ballantine Books, New York, 1991

Higham, Charles, *Kate: The Life of Katharine Hepburn*, Norton, New York, 1975

Kanin, Garson, *Tracy & Hepburn, An Intimate Memoir*, Viking Press, New York, 1970

Laurence Olivier & Vivien Leigh

Coleman, Terry, *Olivier: The Authorised Biography*, Bloomsbury, London, 2005

Edwards, Anne, *Vivien Leigh: A Biography*, Simon & Schuster, London, 1979

Olivier, Laurence, *Confessions of an Actor*, Weidenfeld & Nicolson, London, 1982

Federico Fellini & Giulietta Masina

Alpert, Hollis, *Fellini: A Life*, Paragon House, New York, 1988

Kezich, Tullio, *Federico Fellini: His Life and Work*, Faber & Faber, New York, 2002

New York Times obituary of Giulietta Masina, March 24, 1994

The 100 Best Articles: Giulietta Masina (at http://the100.ru/en/womens/giulietta-masina.html)

Humphrey Bogart & Lauren Bacall

Bacall, Lauren, *By Myself*, HarperCollins Publishers, New York, 1979

Hyams, Joe, *Bogart & Bacall: A Love Story*, Michael Joseph, London, 1975

Meyers, Jeffrey, *Bogart: A Life in Hollywood*, Andre Deutsch, London, 1997

Roberto Rossellini & Ingrid Bergman

Bergman, Ingrid, with Burgess, Alan, *Ingrid Bergman: My Story*, Delacorte Press, New York, 1980

Bondanella, Peter, *The Films of Roberto Rossellini*, Cambridge University Press, New York, 1991

Chandler, Charlotte, *Ingrid*, Simon & Schuster, New York, 2007

Dewe Matthews, Tom. "The Love Pirate," article in *The Guardian*, December 1, 2000

Frank Sinatra & Ava Gardner

Kaplan, James, *Frank: The Voice*, Doubleday, New York, 2010

Lahr, John, *Sinatra*, Random House, New York, 1987

Server, Lee, *Ava Gardner: Nothing is Love*, Macmillan, London, 2006

Turner, John Frayn, *Frank Sinatra*, Taylor Trade Publishing, London, 2004

Yves Montand & Simone Signoret

David, Catherine, *Simone Signoret*, Bloomsbury, London, 1992

Darrach, Brad, "Yves Montand," article for *People Magazine*, May 16, 1988

DeMaio, Patricia A., *Garden of Dreams: The Life of Simone Signoret*, University Press of Mississippi, 2014

Montand, Yves, Hamon, Hervé and Rotman, Patrick, *You See, I Haven't Forgotten*, Alfred A. Knopf, New York, 1992

Arthur Miller & Marilyn Monroe

Bigsby, Christopher, *Arthur Miller: The Definitive Biography*, Weidenfeld & Nicolson, London, 2014

Meyers, Jeffrey, *The Genius and the Goddess*, Hutchinson, London, 2009

Miller, Arthur, *Timebends: A Life*, Grove Press, New York and Bloomsbury, London, 1995

Spoto, Donald, *Marilyn Monroe, The Biography*, Crown Publishers, New York, 2001

Summers, Anthony, *Goddess: The Secret Lives of Marilyn Monroe*, Guild Publishing, London, 1985

Richard Burton & Elizabeth Taylor

Bragg, Melvyn, *Rich: The Life of Richard Burton*, Hodder & Stoughton, London, 2010

Fisher, Eddie, *Been There, Done That*, St Martin's Press, New York and Hutchinson, London, 1999

Heymann, C. David, *Liz: An Intimate Biography of Elizabeth Taylor*, Birch Lane Press, New York, 1995

Kashner, Sam, *Furious Love*, HarperCollins, London, 2012

Wanger, Walter, and Hyams, Joe, *My Life with Cleopatra*, Corgi Books, London, 1963

Steve McQueen & Ali MacGraw

MacGraw, Ali, *Moving Pictures: An Autobiography*, Bantam Books, New York, 1991

Sandford, Christopher, *McQueen: The Biography*, HarperCollins, London, 2002

Toffel, Neile McQueen, *My Husband, My Friend, A Memoir*, AuthorHouse, New York, 2006

Corbis/Bettmann: 16, 40, 49, 160; Mike Stewart/Sygma: 139

Getty Images/20th Century-Fox: 149; Apic: 33, 146; Archive Photos: 119; Chatin/Siccoli-Pool/ **Gamma/Gamma-Rapho:** 151; Ed Clark/Time & Life Pictures: 105; Walter Daran/Time & Life Pictures: 95; Myron Davis/Time & Life Pictures: 66; Evening Standard: 153; Tom Gallagher/NY Daily News Archive: 81; General Photographic Agency: 82; Ernst Haas: 162; Bert Hardy/Picture Post: 127; Hulton Archive: 43, 85, 93, 133; Imagno: 64; John Kobal Foundation: 51, 106B, 108; Keystone-France/Gamma-Keystone: 31, 117, 144; Metro-Goldwyn-Mayer: 72, 73; Michael Ochs Archive: 98; Gjon Mili/Time & Life Pictures: 97; Mondadori Portfolio: 112; MPI: 2, 25; F. Pale Huni/Picture Post/IPC Magazines: 116; Gordon Parks/Time & Life Pictures: 124; Popperfoto: 83; Enrico Sarsini/Time & Life Pictures: 174; Silver Screen Collection: 15, 155; Time & Life Pictures: 6B; Topical Press Agency: 30

Hdec: 67

ImageCollect.com/Globe Photos: 3, 14, 17, 18, 19, 34T, 39, 41, 45, 57, 58, 61, 62, 63, 69, 70T, 70B, 75, 76, 77, 78, 79, 87, 88, 89, 90, 91, 94, 100, 101, 102, 103, 106T, 109, 111, 113, 114, 115, 118, 120, 121, 125, 126, 128, 129, 130T, 130B, 132, 134, 135, 136, 138, 140, 141, 142T, 142B, 143, 145, 147, 148, 150, 152, 154, 157, 158, 159, 161, 163, 164, 165, 166T, 166B, 167, 168, 169, 170, 171, 172, 173, 175, 177, 178T, 178B, 180, 181, 182, 183T, 183B, 184, 185, 187L, 187R

JRibaX: 99

Library of Congress, Washington, D.C: 12, 20L, 20R, 21, 22, 23, 24, 27, 28, 29T, 29B, 34B, 35, 38, 46, 48, 52

Rex Features/Everett Collection: 7, 92, 122, 176